# JUMPSTART!
## ICT

*Also available*

**Jumpstart! Literacy**
Key Stage 2/3 Literacy Games
Pie Corbett
1-84312-102-6


**Jumpstart! Numeracy**
Maths Activities and Games for Ages 5–14
John Taylor
1-84312-264-2

# JUMPSTART!
# ICT

## ICT ACTIVITIES AND GAMES FOR AGES 7–14

## John Taylor

 **David Fulton** Publishers

This edition reprinted 2008 by Routledge
2 Park Square, Milton Park, Abingdon, Oxon, OX14 4RN
Simultaneously published in the USA and Canada by Routledge
270 Madison Avenue, New York, NY 10016

First published in Great Britain in 2006 by David Fulton Publishers

10 9 8 7 6 5 4 3 2

David Fulton Publishers is a division of Granada Learning Limited.

*British Library Cataloguing in Publication Data*
A catalogue record for this book is available from the British Library.

ISBN-10: 1 84312 465 3 (ISBN-13: 9781843124658)

Typeset by FiSH Books, Enfield, Middx.
Printed and bound in Great Britain

# Contents

# Preface

The intention of this book is to give ideas for ICT activities and techniques. There is a plethora of software packages available and these are changing constantly. This diversity is further complicated by the number of versions of the same program that are in use at any one time. It is not possible to produce an up-to-date book that covers all these options.

To get around this problem I have restricted this book to Windows Paint (Section 1) and Microsoft (MS) Office programs (Section 2). This is because every user of a Windows operation system has Paint and most computers also have some version of MS Office as standard.

I have included a glossary and two appendices. Appendix 1 lists the most common *keyboard shortcuts* which work in Windows. Appendix 2 is an 'idiot's guide' to Windows Paint.

Words and phrases in *italics* have been included either in the Glossary or one of the two appendices.

Text in **bold** refers to menus and menu options.

Square brackets have been used to identify specific keys on your keyboard.

All of these activities can be used as starting points and can be developed as necessary using different software packages. You can set a challenge of how to achieve the same or better effect using a more specialised, more expensive program.

The instructions given for each activity are meant to be used as a demonstration to be displayed for the group to see. In some cases it can be helpful to split them up into stages. It can be helpful for students to work collaboratively in pairs before developing ideas and practice independently. Peer support and encouragement makes a great difference to those who feel they have no aptitude for ICT, and reinforces the skills of those who help their fellows. It is all too easy when working independently for a non-confident pupil to lag behind the rest and miss an important step.

Some of the activities could be used, if appropriate, as timed challenges, either with individuals trying to better their previous attempt or as races against the neighbouring pupils or the whole group.

Don't forget that there is seldom only one way to achieve an objective, and your pupils may well know or discover other ways that are just as effective as your way, and possibly quicker. When this happens share their discovery and make a mental note of it to use in lessons with other groups.

Finally, before starting, here is the most useful computer shortcut that you will ever learn:

[Ctrl] [Z]

[Ctrl] [Z] is 'undo'. It will get you out of all sorts of fixes, such as when you have inadvertently deleted part of a file or want to reverse changes you have made. The number of actions you can undo in a sequence will depend upon your program and which generation it is. Using this shortcut is quicker than messing around with the mouse. It should become an instinctive reaction whenever you make an error.

**Keys to symbols used:**

 suitable for beginner student

 suitable for intermediate student

 suitable for advanced student

# Introduction

## CHOOSING SOFTWARE

When you choose to use ICT to carry out a task it is important to select the application most suited to what you wish to achieve.

Word processing programs are designed for handling large amounts of text and have more tricks and tools than any 'normal' user could ever learn. Regular users tend to limit their working knowledge to what fulfils their requirements and only investigate how to do something new when the need arises.

Desktop publishing (DTP) programs are ideal when you wish to combine blocks of text with photographs, images, wordarts, etc. for posters, leaflets, flyers and small publications. However, they can also be useful for designing attractive worksheets and record sheets. DTP programs are also often the quickest and most controllable way of arranging, sizing and printing out digital photographs. Another strength of programs such as MS Publisher is the ability to overlay, align and group together drawn shapes to make simple designs and logos.

Spreadsheet programs are not merely tools for doing the school accounts; they can manipulate words as well as numbers, and each cell can be formatted independently. This makes Excel ideal for designing worksheets, forms, timetables and record sheets. My free teacher resource website (www.johnandgwyn.co.uk) has many downloadable examples of how Excel can be used creatively by teachers.

PowerPoint can be expertly employed for fabulous multimedia presentations; though in novice hands it is often used as little more than an overhead projector. PowerPoint is my program of choice for creating flow charts and to structure diagrams. It gives you a large working area to design, alter and adjust, particularly if you have used 'connectors' to link components together.

MS Paint can appear to be a crude tool compared to the sophistication of some programs, but this is its major strength. It can be used as a secondary application to alter images from other applications and to save them as individual files. For example, if you have designed a logo or letterhead in Publisher or PowerPoint it can be pasted into Paint and saved under a separate filename rather than being part of a larger document.

Don't restrict yourself to using one application at a time; it can be helpful to use a second program to create elements and then paste them into the main file. For example, if you are writing a text-based report that requires tables and charts to be inserted, create them in Excel and *copy/paste* into your Word document. Similarly, flow charts are simpler to construct and modify in PowerPoint before pasting into Word.

## SOME HELPFUL HINTS

### Keyboard shortcuts

Many programs give you keyboard shortcuts which save the bother of moving and clicking the mouse around menus and sub-menus. These shortcuts are to be found when you carry out a task using the mouse.

Before clicking on your chosen task from a menu, look to see if a keyboard shortcut is displayed at the side. Some keyboard shortcuts are specific to the program you're using and only worth learning if you use that particular program a lot. There are, however, a lot of time-saving shortcuts which can be used in most/all Microsoft applications; particularly useful when switching between applications. There is a list of the most common in Appendix 1.

### Drawing shapes

If you need to have parts of an image that are the same or similar, don't waste time drawing them one at a time. The activities Making Faces, House Race and Stacking Up illustrate the advantages of drawing an object once and copying it.

Holding down the [Shift] key when drawing images makes the resulting image regular. Rectangles are restricted to being square, ellipses to being circular and lines to being vertical, horizontal or diagonal. Autoshapes in Word, PowerPoint and Publisher are also affected in this way. In Publisher, [Shift] also restricts text boxes and wordarts to being square.

### Working with images

It is good practice to de-select an image as soon as you have finished working with it (inserting, resizing, moving, etc.) by clicking somewhere else on the screen. In some versions of Publisher, if you insert another image with an existing one selected the new image replaces the one you've left selected.

The position of images (and text boxes) can be finely adjusted in Publisher and PowerPoint using the arrow keys in conjunction with either [Shift] or [Alt], depending upon the application being used. When doing this, increase the magnification to 150 per cent or more for even greater accuracy.

### Alignment

Using 'align objects' can make Publisher and PowerPoint files look much neater. This is particularly the case where you have objects with a border, for example in a flow chart or a form with a group of tick boxes. If the objects are the same size and shape it makes no difference which vertical or horizontal alignment option you choose. However, when the objects are different sizes the alignment choice does make a difference to how your work looks.

When aligning such objects horizontally, the 'center' (or 'middle') option is generally better; though text boxes may look better aligned to the 'top' or 'bottom'. Similarly, with vertical alignment, the 'center' option looks neater in most instances. If you have a column of tick boxes you may find it better to align them to the left. This looks better still if the text (box) relating to the tick boxes is aligned to the right.

If you are making a design from more than one autoshape, e.g. a heart shape inside a circle or square, use the 'center' option both vertically and horizontally, then group the objects together, as described in 3D Shapes.

### Creating transparent images

Sometimes you need to make an image in Paint which will *copy/paste* into another application and retain a transparent background that doesn't obscure parts of an adjacent image already in the other file. You may also wish to save your new image as a transparent GIF file. Unfortunately, the 'save as GIF' option does not preserve transparency, even when *Draw opaque* is disabled. To further complicate matters, when you load a transparent GIF into Paint it appears with a black background. Here is the solution: make your design and *copy/paste* it into PowerPoint. With your image selected, click on the **Set transparent color** icon (on the

**Picture** toolbar), then click on the background area of your image. This will now *copy/paste* with a transparent background. To save it and retain the transparent background, right-click on it, select **Save as picture**, and save it as a GIF (Graphics Interchange Format) file.

### Stretch, rotate, skew and crop handles

Handles are the points on an object which you can drag on to alter it. In Publisher and PowerPoint they are coloured to indicate what they are for. The white stretch handles are round in shape and positioned in the centre of the top, bottom and sides and at the corners. When resizing, use a corner handle in order to maintain the image's proportions. Using a top, bottom or side handle adjusts only one dimension, distorting the image. The *rotate handle* is round and green. Dragging on it allows you to rotate the object. In earlier versions of Publisher rotation is done via the rotate icon on the toolbar or the **Arrange** menu.

Where applicable, the *skew handle* is yellow and diamond-shaped. It allows you to adjust some autoshapes. In earlier versions of Publisher the *skew handle* is grey.

Crop handles appear when a cropable object is selected and the crop icon is clicked. In the centre of each edge they appear as a short, bold line, parallel with the edge, with a shorter line projecting outwards at right-angles from its centre. Corner crop handles appear as a bold right-angle.

### Format painter

This editing tool is available on 2000-onwards versions of Excel, Publisher, PowerPoint and Word. It is particularly useful when working on text documents that have multiple fonts, sizes and styles, and when you have pasted text in from another file. Format painter enables you to use an existing section of text and apply its format to another section. In Excel it allows you to give other cells exactly the same format as another. To use format painter, copy part of the text or cell onto the clipboard, click on the format painter icon and drag the cursor over the section you wish to change.

### Print screen

This key copies an image of the entire screen onto the clipboard. You can then paste it into a document and crop off from all four edges, leaving you with the section you want. Alternatively, paste it into Paint, press [Esc], use one of the two *select* tools to grab the bit you want, then either paste into another file or use **Edit/Copy to...** to save it as a file in its own right. This technique is particularly useful where you need to grab part of an image from a non-Office computer program, such as a game or specialist educational software. Capture a Card Suit uses this technique. On a standard keyboard the key is located between the main and number keypads. On laptops it generally comes after the last function key and its label is often abbreviated to [Prt Scrn] or similar.

### Make it relevant

Computer users tend only to remember how to use the tools and options that are useful for achieving their normal tasks. We can be shown how to do something 'clever', but if it serves no useful purpose in our day-to-day usage we forget how to do it. This is no great problem, as long as when you need to use it, (a) you remember that it can be done, and (b) you are competent at searching the help files on- or off-line.

So it is important that computer software techniques are useful, relevant and related to a specific task or need. Design flyers or posters to promote a real event, make leaflets to inform about a real issue or service. If learning to use formulae on a spreadsheet (see Invoice Generator) use real objects and prices.

## Can it be done better?

When a task has been completed, review how well the task has been achieved. Was the software used appropriate? Could another program achieve the same effect better or easier? Had time allowed, how could it have been improved? If the task were to be repeated, would you do it the same way? Can the techniques be used for another task?

# Windows Paint Activities

Everyone who uses MS Windows has Windows Paint as one of its accessories. It's basic and simple to use but also very useful. For instance, if a clipart you've found isn't quite right for a DTP document, paste it into Paint, modify as required and paste it back again.

While the instructions below are specific to Windows Paint, the activities themselves could also be done using many alternative graphics programs such as Corel Draw. Having completed an activity in Paint, you could set your pupils the task of replicating it in a more sophisticated program.

## MAKING WAVES

*OBJECTIVE: TO MAKE WAVE PATTERNS*

**Tools and skills involved**
*Ellipse* tool with [Shift] held down to draw concentric circles
*Select* tool with *Draw opaque* disabled
[Ctrl] *drag* technique to copy

**What to do**
- Click on the *Ellipse* tool, then, while holding down [Shift], *drag* out a circle.
- Click on the standard (rectangular) *select* tool, and make sure that the *Draw opaque* is disabled. This is done either from the **Image** menu or by clicking the

lower of the two buttons below the ellipse tool button. Drag it horizontally across the centre of the circle then downwards to select the lower half of the circle.

- Placing the cursor over the selected area, *drag* it to the right and join the left end of the lower half to the right end of the upper half.
- Select the two joined half-circles by dragging around them.
- Hold down [Ctrl] and pause a moment before dragging a copy and joining it on to the end.
- Now select both parts and drag another copy onto the end.

### Variations

- Use different colours – before joining on a section of wave, use the *Fill with color* tool to change its colour before joining on.
- Use [Ctrl] *drag* to make a copy of the wave beneath the first and flip it vertically (this is done via the **Image** menu).
- Use different line thicknesses – click the line tool button, select a thicker line then click the *Ellipse* tool.

## MAKING BORDERS

*OBJECTIVE: TO MAKE A BORDER USING ONE'S OWN PATTERN*

### Tools and skills involved
*Ellipse* with [Shift] held to draw concentric circles
*Select* tool with *Draw opaque* disabled
[Ctrl] *drag* technique to copy
Rotating a selected part of an image

### What to do
- Make a wave as described above.

- [Ctrl] *drag* a copy, and while it is still 'selected', click on the **Image** menu, click **Flip/rotate** and choose **Rotate by angle/90°**.
- Join your rotated wave to one end of the horizontal wave.
- Complete the other two sides by [Ctrl] *dragging* from the first two waves.

**Variations**
- Use solid shapes – with the *Ellipse* tool selected, click on the bottom of the three rectangular buttons that appear on the toolbar when the shape tools are chosen.
- Make square waves (castellations) by starting off with the rectangle tool instead of the *Ellipse* tool.
- Use different colours.
- Make a double border, as below.

## MAKING DOUBLE BORDERS

*OBJECTIVE: TO MAKE A BORDER USING ONE'S OWN PATTERN*

**Tools and skills involved**
As above plus:
[Ctrl] [C] and [Ctrl] [V] shortcuts
Resizing
*Fill with color*

**What to do**
- Make a single border as described above.
- Select the single border and copy it to the clipboard using [Ctrl] [C].
- Paste in a copy using [Ctrl] [V], and with the pasted copy still highlighted, resize the new copy by dragging on the *handles*, making it smaller or larger than the original.

- While the resized copy is still selected, move it over to form a double border.

**Variations**
- Use the *Fill with color* tool to colour the space between the two borders. When doing this you must make sure you haven't left gaps in the corners, otherwise the colour will flood out, filling the screen. If this happens use [Ctrl] [Z] to undo, then zoom in using the *Magnify* tool and fill the gap.

## HOW STEADY IS YOUR HAND?

*OBJECTIVE: TO PRACTISE FINE MOUSE MOVEMENT*

**Tools and skills involved**
*Text*
*Brush*
*Pencil*

**What to do**
- Choose the *Text* tool and drag out a text box. When you do this the text toolbar should appear. If it does not, switch it on from the **View** menu.
- Type in a word, group of letters or numerals.
- While the text box is still active you can change the font and text size using the text toolbar and the colour by using the *Color box*. To go higher than size 72, highlight the size displayed, type in your new size and press [Enter].
- Click on *Brush*, choose a brush size and shape, and a different colour. Draw over the top of the letters, trying to remain exactly in the centre. Each time you go off-line use [Ctrl] [Z] to undo.

**Variations**
- Trace over with the *pencil*.

- Use a smaller font size to begin with.
- Get pairs or groups to race each other using the same letters and font size. Disqualify anyone who goes outside the typed letters.

## SYMMETRICAL NAMES

*OBJECTIVE: TO INTRODUCE VERTICAL AND HORIZONTAL FLIP*

**Tools and skills involved**
*Text*
*Flip*
*Fill with color*
*Select* tool with *Draw opaque* disabled

**What to do**
- Use *Text* (size 72) to write a name.
- Click on *select* and select the name.
- Use [Ctrl] *drag* to make a copy beneath the original and *flip* it vertically (go to **View** menu for flip options).
- Change colour(s) using *Fill with color*.
- Re-select the flipped name and place it beneath the original, as a mirrored image.

**Variations**
- Make a copy of the name and its reflection to the right and *flip* it horizontally.
- Flip the original copy of the name horizontally and place at the side instead of beneath.
- Save the finished design by selecting it, then click on the **Edit** menu and the **Copy to...** option to save just the finished design rather than the whole page.

# TILES 1

*OBJECTIVE: TO MAKE A TILE WITH ONE LINE OF SYMMETRY*

**Tools and skills involved**
*Rectangle*
*Curve*
*Fill with color* tool
[Ctrl] *drag*
[Ctrl] [C] and [Ctrl] [V] shortcuts
*Flip*
*Select* tool with *Draw opaque* disabled

**What to do**
- Use *Rectangle* to drag out a vertical oblong about 200 pixels tall and 100 wide. Most versions of Paint display the dimensions in pixels in the bottom right corner of the screen as you drag out.
- Choose *Curve* and drag down from the top right corner to the bottom right, then click to the left to curve it. A second click will lock the curve; if this is not done in the same place it produces a second curve in the line. If you wish, add another curved line linking the left side of the oblong to the first curve.
- Make sure corners meet then use the *Fill with color* tool.
- Outline the oblong using the *select* tool and make a copy EITHER using [Ctrl] *drag* method OR by using [Ctrl] [C] and [Ctrl] [V] shortcuts to copy and paste.
- With the copy still selected, *flip* it horizontally (use the **Image** menu then **Flip/rotate**).
- Join the two oblongs together.
- You may wish to remove the centre join by brushing out the lines with the colours used for filling in.

13

**Variations**
- Copy the tile to the clipboard then paste in tiles and arrange them in rows, leaving just enough space for the grouting.
- Tile the screen but rotate alternate tiles 180°.

## TILES 2

*OBJECTIVE: TO MAKE A TILE WITH TWO LINES OF SYMMETRY*

**Tools and skills involved**
*Rectangle*
*Curve*
[Ctrl] *drag*
*Fill with color*
[Ctrl] [C] and [Ctrl] [V] shortcuts
*Flip*
*Select* tool with *Draw opaque* disabled

**What to do**
- Choose the *Rectangle* tool, and while holding down [Shift], *drag* out a square around 150 pixels width.
- Divide up the inside of the square using shapes, lines or curves and colour the sections using the *Fill with colour* tool.
- Make a copy of the decorated square, *flip* it *horizontally* and join it on to the right-hand side of the first.
- Select these two joined squares, copy them, *flip* them *vertically* and join them beneath the first pair.
- If you wish, select the whole new symmetrical tile and save it using the **Edit** menu and **Copy to . . . .**

**Variations**
- Copy the tile to the clipboard then paste in tiles and arrange them in rows, leaving just enough space for the grouting.

- Tile the screen but rotate alternate tiles 180°.

## RAINBOW PAINTBRUSH

*OBJECTIVE: TO MAKE AND USE A STRIPED PAINTBRUSH*

**Tools and skills involved**
*Brush*
[Shift] *drag*
*Select* tool with *Draw opaque* disabled

**What to do**
- Choose the largest square *Brush*. (Brush shapes and sizes appear on the toolbar when *Brush* is activated.)
- Choose a colour, e.g. red, and click once on the drawing area to produce one small red square.
- Change to another colour and click immediately below the first square.
- Repeat until you have a column of six or seven different colours.
- *Select* the coloured squares, dragging the selection tool as close as you can to the edges of the column.
- Save a copy onto the clipboard using [Ctrl] [C].
- Hold down the [Shift] key, pause a moment, and then with the cursor over the selection, *drag*. You're painting with a striped brush.

**Variations**
- Write your name in striped paint – at the end of each letter, let go of the [Shift] key then move the selected coloured squares to the starting point for the next letter before holding [Shift] down again.
- Move the mouse quicker to produce a staggered painting effect.
- Make other shaped multi-coloured brushes by placing dots or squares of colour around in a small circle or square.

## MAKING FACES 1

*OBJECTIVE: TO BUILD UP A FACE*

**Tools and skills involved**
*Ellipse*
*Fill with color*
*Pencil*
[Ctrl] *drag* (to copy)
*Select* tool with *Draw opaque* disabled
*Erase*
*Airbrush*

**What to do**
- Use *Ellipse* to draw an ellipse (outside of eye) and two circles for the iris and pupil – holding down [Shift] as you drag will make them concentric.
- Use *select* to place the pupil circle in the centre of the iris, then the whole eyeball into the ellipse.
- Use *Fill with color* to colour pupil and iris.
- Choose *Pencil* and right-click a couple of times just above the centre of the pupil to give the impression of reflection. Set the pencil colour to red and draw in a few veins on the sclera (the white bit).
- Select the whole eye and [Ctrl] *drag* to make a copy of it.
- Make a nose by drawing two ellipses, one 'portrait' and one 'landscape'. Overlay them, then use *Erase* to remove the sections of line in the centre.
- For the mouth, start with two ellipses of the same width (use the width in pixels displayed bottom right as a guide), both very thin but one thinner than the other.
- *Select* and [Delete] the top half of each ellipse, then overlay the residual curves with ends touching. Colour the lip using *Fill with color*.
- If you wish, [Ctrl] *drag* a copy above the first lip and flip it vertically, joining the two to make a more realistic mouth.

- Draw a large ellipse for the main head, move the face parts into position (if not already done) and use the *Airbrush* to spray on some hair.

**Variations**
- Vary colours shapes, sizes.
- Challenge pupils to draw a more realistic nose.
- Position the eyeball to one side of the sclera, then select both eyes and *flip* them horizontally to make the face look the other way. Use [Ctrl] [Z] to undo this flip.

## MAKING FACES 2

*OBJECTIVE: TO BUILD UP A FACE USING FONT CHARACTERS*

**Tools and skills involved**
*Text* with the Webdings font
*Ellipse*
*Fill with color*
*Pencil*
[Ctrl] *drag* (to copy)
*Select* with *Draw opaque* disabled
*Erase*
*Airbrush*

**What to do**
- Choose *Text* and make a text box with the Webdings font in size 72. Type a capital N followed by a capital O. This will give you one eye and a left ear.
- If you wish, re-colour using *Fill with color*.
- Make copies of them using [Ctrl] *drag* or [Ctrl] [C] and [Ctrl] [V], and *flip* one ear horizontally.
- Use a *Text* box sized about 144 with a normal font (e.g. Arial, Comic Sans) and type a zero or capital O.
- Choose *select* and make a copy, and *rotate* one copy 90° to use as a mouth.

- Use the other one for a nose.
- Use *Ellipse* for the face shape and assemble the parts, and spray on some hair with the *Airbrush*.

### Variations
- Vary colours shapes, sizes.
- Stretch the mouth – choose *select*, drag a box around it and pull on one of the side *handles* of the select box.
- Make a nose from two copies of the letter, one rotated 90° and joined together as described in Making Faces 1.

## HOUSE RACE

*OBJECTIVE: TO BUILD UP A HOUSE IN UNDER A MINUTE*

### Tools and skills involved
*Rectangle*
*Fill with color*
*Line* (with [Shift] held down)
[Ctrl] *drag* (to copy)
*Select* with *Draw opaque* disabled
[Ctrl] [C] and [Ctrl] [V] shortcuts
*Flip*

### What to do
- Use *Rectangle* to draw an oblong about 100 pixels wide and 50 deep.
- *Drag* a *select box* around the oblong and [Ctrl] *drag* a copy to the right, but leave it overlapping with the original giving the appearance of a window with a central, large pane with narrower panes either side.
- [Ctrl] *drag* a copy of this window over to the right, but leave a space for a smaller window to go in between.

- [Ctrl] *drag* a copy of these two windows below for downstairs.
- *Drag* a *select box* around the larger pane of one of the windows and [Ctrl] *drag* a copy to the space between the upstairs windows.
- Use *Rectangle* to make an oblong door. Keep the top of it level with the top of the downstairs windows. Now surround the windows with an oblong front wall, with the top just fractionally above the top of the upstairs windows.
- Chose *Line* and position the cursor on one of the top corners of the wall. Hold down [Shift] and draw a diagonal line, stopping before you reach the top of the drawing area. Draw a horizontal line (holding down [Shift]) from the upper end of the diagonal and end it just past half way across the house.
- *Drag* a *select box* around these two lines, use [Ctrl] [C] and [Ctrl] [V] to paste in a copy which can then be flipped horizontally and aligned to form the rest of the roof.
- If you have space add on a chimney.
- Quickly colour in using *Fill with color*.

Yes, this can really be done in less than a minute!

### Variations
- Use a timer and allow half the group one minute to draw a house. Compare the finished results, then allow the other half to do the same. Whose efforts are closest to the brief?
- Set criteria for a house (number of windows, smoke out of chimney, etc.) and try again.

# THE SQUARES GAME 1

*OBJECTIVE: TO PRACTISE USE OF THE SELECT TOOL*

**Tools and skills involved**
*Rectangle* with [Shift]
[Ctrl] *drag*
*Select* with *Draw opaque* enabled
*Fill with color*

**What to do**
- Use *Rectangle* with [Shift] held down to draw a square measuring about 40 pixels.
- Make 14 copies of the square and arrange them in five columns of 1, 2, 3, 4 and 5 squares, rather like a set of skittles.
- Use *Fill with color* to give each column of squares its own colour.
- The Squares Game is played by two people taking turns at selecting squares and deleting them with the [Delete] key.
- To play the game there are only two rules:
  Rule 1: When it's your turn you may delete as many squares as you like that are the same colour (i.e. in the same column).
  Rule 2: The winner is the player who leaves the other player the last square.
- While playing the game, a number of winning patterns will become apparent, such as leaving your opponent two pairs of squares.

**Variations**
- To save time, save your file before commencing play.
- Copy the set of squares to the clipboard, ready to be pasted in for the next game.

# THE CIRCLES GAME

*OBJECTIVE: TO PRACTISE USE OF THE* FREE-FORM SELECT *TOOL WHILE PLAYING A QUICK AND SIMPLE STRATEGY GAME*

**Tools and skills involved**
*Ellipse* with [Shift]
[Ctrl] *drag*
*Free-form select*

**What to do**

- Choose *Ellipse* and select solid fill by clicking on the bottom of the three fill boxes on the toolbar. Choose a bright colour, then, while holding down [Shift], drag out five circles of varying size.
- Change colour and draw five more circles of varied size. Repeat with two or three more colours.
- Save the file for future use.
- Use [Ctrl] [A] to *select all* and [Ctrl] [C] to copy it to the clipboard ready to paste back in for another game.
- The game is played using the *Free-form select* tool to select a group of circles, and the [Delete] key to remove them.
- There are three rules:
  Rule 1: When it is your turn you can select and remove as many circles of the same colour as yours. You can restart the selecting process but can only press [Delete] once during a turn.
  Rule 2: If a circle of another colour gets included accidentally when you remove your selection, you lose.
  Rule 3: The winner is the player who leaves the last circle behind for the other player.
- As with the Squares Game, winning patterns will become apparent, such as leaving 1 of one colour, 2 of another and 3 of a third.

**Variations**
- Work in pairs; the loser swaps places with the winner from another pair.
- Pairs swap computers and use another pair's set of circles.
- Increase the number of sets of circles.
- Encourage the strategic positioning of different coloured circles closely together to make mouse control difficult, and the odd small circle 'hidden' in a corner, ready to be overlooked.

# THE CIRCLES CHALLENGE

*OBJECTIVE: TO PRACTISE USE OF THE* FREE-FORM SELECT *TOOL AGAINST THE CLOCK*

**Tools and skills involved**
*Ellipse* with [Shift] held down as you drag
[Ctrl] *drag*
*Free-form select*

**What to do**
- The challenge is for each member of a pair, in turn, to set the other a circles challenge to be tackled against the clock.
- The challenge setter needs to draw sets of coloured circles as described in The Circles Game. Their aim is to make it as awkward as possible. The set of circles must be saved and copied to the clipboard prior to starting the challenge.
- The player who is challenged must remove all the circles of one colour in one select and delete operation, i.e. all the red circles must be deleted with one press of the [Delete] key.
- They must then remove the other colour sets in the same way. If they fail to remove all of a colour in one go, or include a circle of a different colour, they must start again, but the timer continues.

- The two players swap roles. The player who completes the challenge set in the shorter time is judged the winner.

**Variations**

- Work in pairs; the loser swaps places with the winner from another pair.
- Instead of restarting from an error, add a ten-second penalty to the time.
- Increase the number of sets of circles.
- Use a variety of shapes, selecting either: all the shapes of one colour; all the same shape; or all of the same shape and colour.

# THE ICON FLIP CHALLENGE

*OBJECTIVE: TO COPY AND PASTE THE SCREEN CONTENTS INTO WINDOWS PAINT (OR ANOTHER GRAPHICS PROGRAM), THEN FLIP OVER THE PROGRAM ICONS*

**Tools and skills involved**
[Print screen] key (usually located to the right of the [Enter] key on a normal keyboard, and to the right of the function keys on a laptop)
*Select* with *Draw opaque* disabled
*Flip*

**What to do**

- Begin with everyone's computer screen displaying your normal desktop with program icons.
- Press the [Print screen] button (note the words may be abbreviated), which will copy the entire screen contents to the clipboard.
- Open Windows Paint and paste in the clipboard contents.
- *Select* individual icons and *flip* them over horizontally.

- Make everyone start together and see who is the quickest to flip them all, one at a time. Selecting a group of icons together would move their relative positions.

**Variations**
- Choose one icon and paste copies of it (without text beneath) over each of the other icons.
- Rotate icons.
- Select an icon, hold down [Shift] and use it as a paintbrush (as described in Rainbow Paintbrush).

## CELEBRITY STRETCH

*OBJECTIVE: TO DISTORT A PHOTOGRAPH BY USING [SHIFT] DRAG IN CONJUNCTION WITH FREE-FORM SELECT TO STRETCH LIMBS, NECK, HEAD, TORSO, ETC.*

You will need a few suitable photographs of 'celebrities' possibly from web-searching. The ideal should have them standing facing the camera, with at least one arm and hand visible.

**Tools and skills involved**
Internet image search
*Free-form select*
[Shift] *drag* with *Draw opaque* disabled

**What to do**
- Load the celebrity's picture into Windows Paint.
- Use *Free-form select* to trace all around the head and straight across the neck. This needs to be done carefully, perhaps using a second hand to guide the mouse.
- With the cursor over the selected head, hold down [Shift] and pause for a moment before gently raising the head upwards. The bottom section of

the selected area will act as a paintbrush, stretching the neck out. If you wobble too much, use [Ctrl] [Z] to undo and try again. If you want the 'just escaped from an alien spaceship' effect, try a long wobbly neck.

- Select an arm or two and do the same; extra-long arms can look quite comical.
- The torso is also worth the stretch treatment.
- Highlight the finished object with *Free-form select* then save just that part of the image by going to the **Edit** menu and choosing **Copy to ....**
- Paste several re-designed celebrities into a new picture using **Paste from ...** from the **Edit** menu. You may wish to insert them into a different program such as MS Publisher.

### Variations

- Use a picture of yourself.
- Invite volunteers to work on digital pictures of themselves.
- The celebrity 'holy grail' would be a photograph of a famous footballer about to take a throw in, with hands above his head. You may have to resize the head slightly to fit in the space of the ball!

## FACE PAINT

*OBJECTIVE: TO USE A SELECTED PART OF A PHOTOGRAPH AS A PAINTBRUSH USING [SHIFT] DRAG IN CONJUNCTION WITH FREE-FORM SELECT*

You will need a few suitable photographs, possibly from web-searching or the last school social function or class photo.

### Tools and skills involved
*Free-form select*
[Shift] *drag* with *Draw opaque* disabled

**What to do**

- Load the photograph into Windows Paint.
- Use *Free-form select* to trace all around the head. This needs to be done very accurately, perhaps using the other hand to guide the mouse. Avoid picking up part of the background, yet also try not to cut off an ear.
- As a precaution, save the selected head by going to the **Edit** menu and choosing **Copy to . . . .**
- Copy the head onto the clipboard and open a new file. [Ctrl] [N] will save you having to use **New** from the **File** menu.
- Paste in the face using [Ctrl] [V].
- With the cursor over the selected head, hold down [Shift] and pause for a moment, then gently move the mouse. Each time you pass the mouse over the trail of 'face paint' it creates a 3D effect. Moving the mouse very quickly will leave a space between each image.

**Variations**

- Use a picture of yourself.
- If the face image is small enough, try writing a name or word in 'face paint'.

## HEAD SWAP

*OBJECTIVE: TO USE TWO LIVE WINDOWS WITH WINDOWS PAINT RUNNING TO SWAP HEADS ABOUT*

You will need a few suitable photographs, ideally formal poses, featuring at least two people. Team photographs work well and are easy to find on the web using a team name as a search phrase in an *Advanced search*. Alternatively, search for the current publicity-chasing 'celebrity couple'.

### Tools and skills involved

*Free-form select*

[Shift] *drag* with *Draw opaque* disabled

### What to do

- Open TWO windows with Windows Paint running and load the photograph into both.
- Use *Free-form select* to trace all around a head in one Paint window. Accuracy is important; you don't want background included.
- Copy the head onto the clipboard and switch to the second Paint window.
- Paste the face onto someone else's body using [Ctrl] [V].
- Return to the first Paint window and collect another head and transfer this onto someone else in the second Paint window.

### Variations

- Use a picture of yourself and stick it on a sport celebrity's body.
- If the face is turned slightly to one side, try a horizontal flip.

## SYMMETRICAL HEADS 1

*OBJECTIVE: TO CREATE TWO NEW SYMMETRICAL IMAGES USING EACH SIDE OF A PHOTOGRAPH OF SOMEONE'S FACE*

Photographs need to show a face more or less square on to the camera. If the face is looking slightly to one side, the difference between the resulting images is exaggerated, often with amusing results. You can use pupil and staff photographs taken especially for the purpose, or the internet to find pictures of celebrities.

*See also* Symmetrical Heads 2 in Section 2.

**Tools and skills involved**
*Free-form select*
*Select*
[Shift] *drag* with *Draw opaque* disabled
*Flip*
[Ctrl] [C] and [Ctrl] [V]

**What to do**
- Load your 'donor photograph' into Windows Paint.
- Carefully trace around the face with the *Free-form select* tool, then copy it to the clipboard using [Ctrl] [C]. You may also wish to save a copy of this cut-out by going to the **Edit** menu and selecting **Copy to . . . .**
- Open a new file (you can use the shortcut [Ctrl] [N] to do this if you like) and paste in the face using [Ctrl] [V].
- Make sure that *Draw opaque* is disabled. Click on *select* and *drag* the start of a *select box* down through the centre of the person's nose, then out to the side. It may well take several attempts to get the side of the *select box* exactly through the centre of the face.
- *Drag* one half of the face downwards so that it is below where it was, leaving a couple of vertical centimetres between it and the other half.
- With the one half still selected [Ctrl] *drag* a copy next to the 'cut' side, flip it horizontally (use the **Image** menu to access the *flip* tool), and join the two parts together.
- Select the other half and repeat the copy, flip and join routine, giving you a second symmetrical image.
- Rearrange the two new 'faces' side by side and paste alongside the original face.
- Save and/or print out as you wish.

**Variations**
- Experiment with faces that are not completely square on to the camera.
- Try faces that are tilted slightly to one side.

## SHAPE RACE 1

*OBJECTIVE: TO ENCOURAGE USE OF DIFFERENT TECHNIQUES TO DRAW PRESCRIBED OBJECTS FASTER*

It is also a test of who has remembered how to use tools and short cuts.

*See also* Shape Race 2 in Section 2.

### Tools and skills involved
*Free-form select*
[Shift] *drag* with *Draw opaque* disabled
[Ctrl] [C] and [Ctrl] [V]
*Rectangle* and *Ellipse* with and without [Shift] held

### What to do
- This can be done either by pupils at adjacent computers, racing each other, or else by having the first to achieve the task raise both hands and call out that they have finished.
- Everyone must begin with hands on heads, waiting for you to call out what they have to draw, at which point the race is on.
- You call out the task, for example: 'Five red (i.e. filled) oblongs, two blue circles and three squares', etc.
- When you have checked that the first one to complete the task has indeed achieved it, they drop out and take on a supervisory role.
- To make the selection easier you could use the Excel-based random shape selector file as described in Shape Race 2 in Section 2.

### Variations
- Specify whether shapes should be hollow or filled.
- Specify colour(s).
- Specify more than one set of shapes.
- Specify the approximate size of shapes according to an agreed range, e.g. 'small' = less than 4 cm; 'large' = more than 10 cm.

## OPTICAL ILLUSIONS 1

*OBJECTIVE: TO CREATE A SIMPLE CONCAVE/CONVEX OPTICAL ILLUSION USING CIRCLES*

**Tools and skills involved**
*Ellipse* with [Shift] held and no fill
Select with *Draw opaque* disabled
[Ctrl] *drag*
*Fill with color*
**Edit colors/Define custom color**

**What to do**
- Hold down [Shift] as you use *Ellipse* to draw a series of circles with diameters of 30, 50, 70, 90, 110, 130, 150 and 170 pixels. As you drag out the circles, the diameter in pixels should be displayed in the bottom right-hand corner, next to the cursor position co-ordinates. Arrange them along the top of the drawing area.
- Place the second largest circle inside the largest so that the tops of both circles are touching. In descending order of size, move the other circles inside with the tops of all the circles meeting.
- What does it look like: the inside of a pipe or tunnel; a truncated cone viewed from one side?
- Make a few copies using [Ctrl] *drag*. Use *Fill with color* to colour the rings of one in random colours. With another copy use progressively darker or lighter tints of the same colour. To change tints, select a colour from the *Color box*, choose **Edit colors...** from the **Color** menu, and select **Define custom color**. Use the tone slider on the right to darken or lighten, then click OK. When you have filled with one tint use the slider to change it a little more.
- Do progressive tints affect how you see the illusion?

**Variations**
- Use ellipses.

## OPTICAL ILLUSIONS 2

*OBJECTIVE: TO CREATE A SIMPLE CONCAVE/ CONVEX OPTICAL ILLUSION USING SQUARES*

**Tools and skills involved**
*Rectangle* with [Shift] held and no fill
*Select* with *Draw opaque* disabled
[Ctrl] [C] and [Ctrl] [V]
[Ctrl] *drag*
*Fill with color*
*Line*
**Edit colors/Define custom color**

**What to do**
- Hold down [Shift] as you use *Rectangle* to draw a series of squares with sides of 20, 40, 60, 80, 100 and 120 pixels. As you drag out the squares, the size in pixels should be displayed in the bottom right-hand corner, next to the cursor position co-ordinates. Arrange them along the top of the drawing area.
- Use [Ctrl] [C] to copy the squares to the clipboard.
- Place all the squares centralised on top of each other. What do they resemble?
- [Ctrl] *drag* a copy, then add diagonal lines joining each corner of the smallest square to the corresponding corner of the largest.
- Paste in a second set of squares from the clipboard using [Ctrl] [V]. Place these on top of each other, centred left to right but with the top edges touching.
- Make a copy of this set and add diagonal lines linking only the bottom corners of the smallest square to the bottom corners of the largest.

- Colour in each set of squares.
- Is the illusion affected by alignment, the extra diagonal lines or the colour schemes?

**Variations**
- Use rectangles.

## COLOUR MIX & MATCH

*OBJECTIVE: TO EDIT COLOURS TO MATCH THE COLOUR OF AN ARBITRARY OBJECT AND COMPARE ON-SCREEN VERSION WITH PRINT OUT*

**Tools and skills involved**
*Rectangle* with fill
**Edit color/Define custom colors**

**What to do**
- Choose arbitrary items as colour samples – text- or exercise-book covers, school tie, classroom decor, etc.
- Click on the **Color** menu and go to **Edit color**, then **Define custom colors**.
- Find the approximate shade you are after on the colour matrix, then fine-tune the luminosity using the slider. When you think you have a good match, click on **Add to custom colors**, then click **OK**.
- Use *Rectangle* with fill (the third fill option displayed beneath the shape tool buttons), and drag out a rectangle of your custom colour. If your sample is portable hold it against your screen to compare  the colour. If the match is not good, go back to **Define custom colors** and adjust it, then try again.
- When you are happy with the on-screen match, print out a rectangle on a colour printer and compare this with the original sample and the screen image.

**Variations**
- Use a variety of colour samples and consult others on whether or not the match is good.
- Do males and females agree about colour matches? What names do people give to describe the colours and shades.

# MS Office Activities

The instructions below are specific to MS Office programs. The activities in this section can also be done using alternative software, though there will be variations in precisely how to achieve the same results. There are a number of versions of each program in common use and this is likely to increase. It is inevitable therefore that the instructions given here may vary slightly in some versions. If this should arise, you should be able to find the solution from help files.

## RANDOM SENTENCE MAKER

*OBJECTIVE: TO USE RANDOM NUMBER GENERATION AND THE **IF** FUNCTION TO CREATE SENTENCES WHICH CHANGE EACH TIME THE [F9] KEY IS PRESSED*

**Programs and functions involved**
MS Excel
**=RANDBETWEEN**(<value>,<value>)
**=IF** function

**What to do**
- For your demonstration it is safer to have the file described below ready, tested and saved.
- Open up a blank spreadsheet and enter the following into specified cells:
  - In cells A1 and B1 insert: **=RANDBETWEEN(1,5)**. Note: To use the RANDBETWEEN function you must have the **Analysis Toolpak** enabled. To do

this go to the **Tools** menu and click on **Add-Ins....**

o In each of cells A4 to A8 enter the plural names of five creatures: (e.g. cats, sharks, children, chickens, birds). Highlight the cells with a background colour and/or borders.

o In each of cells B4 to B8 enter a word or phrase that would describe what the creature in the adjoining cell likes to do (e.g. sleep, bite people, ride bikes, cross the road, fly). Again highlight the cells.

o Into cell B5 insert: =IF(A1=1,A4,IF (A1=2,A5,IF(A1=3,A6,IF (A1=4,A7,A8)))).

o Justify B5 to the right.

o Increase the font of cells B5 to D5 to size 16.

o In C5 write: **like to.**

o In D5 insert: =IF(B1=1,B4,IF(B1=2,B5,IF (B1=3,B6,IF(B1=4,B7,B8)))).

o Each time you press the [F9] key a new sentence will be generated.

**Variations**

• Change the contents of cells A4 to A8 and B4 to B8.

• Make a random sentence maker of your own, but be aware of what some imaginative adolescents might include!

• Add extra creatures and habits by raising the number range in cells A1 and B1, then add more **IF**s to the formulae in cells B5 and D5. Note 1: When you add another **IF** you must add a close bracket at the end to match the extra open bracket. Note 2: Your last cell reference in the formula comes straight after the penultimate one.

## SHAPE RACE 2

*OBJECTIVE: TO ENCOURAGE USE OF DIFFERENT TECHNIQUES TO DRAW A PRESCRIBED SET OF OBJECTS ALIGNED VERTICALLY OR HORIZONTALLY*

**Programs and functions involved**
MS Publisher or MS PowerPoint
[Shift] *drag*
[Ctrl] [C] and [Ctrl] [V]
*Rectangle* and *Ellipse* tools with and without [Shift] held

MS Excel
**=RANDBETWEEN**(<value>,<value>)
**=IF** function

**What to do**
- This is organised in the same way as in Shape Race 1. The major differences are:
  (a) it uses Publisher or PowerPoint;
  (b) it introduces alignment and size ordering;
  (c) you use an Excel file displayed on your data projector to randomly generate what you want them to draw.
- To make the Excel file, make sure that the **Analysis Toolpak** is enabled. To do this go to the **Tools** menu and click on **Add-Ins . . . .**
- Put the following into the cells specified below:
  - In cells B1, B5 and C1: **=RANDBETWEEN(2,5)**
  - In cells D1 and E1: **= RANDBETWEEN(1,3)**
  - In cell C5: **= IF(B1=2,'red',IF(B1=3,'blue', IF(B1=4,'yellow',IF(B1=5,'green','black'))))**
  - In cell D5: **= IF(C1=2,'squares',IF(C1=3,'oblongs', IF(C1=4,'circles',IF(C1=5,'ellipses','triangles'))))**
  - In cell C7: **= IF(D1=1,'in a row',IF(D1=2,'in a column','scattered about'))**
  - In cell C9: **= IF(E1=1,'all the same size',IF(E1=2,'getting smaller','getting bigger')).**

Increase the font size for cells C5, D5, C7 and C9 –
you may have to widen columns. Each time you
press the [F9] the task will automatically change.

- To align objects in **Publisher** select them by dragging
around or by holding [Ctrl] as you click them, then
go to the **Arrange** menu and choose **Align objects**.
- To align objects in **PowerPoint** select them by
dragging around or by holding [Shift] as you click
them, then click on **Draw** (on the Drawing toolbar)
and choose **Align** or **distribute**.

### Variations

- Change the shapes or colours specified in the IF
statements.
- Add to the IF statements, but remember:
Note 1: You will need to increase the number range
in some of the RANDBETWEEN statements.
Note 2: When you add another **IF** you must add a
close bracket at the end to match the extra open
bracket.
Note 3: Your last cell reference in the formula
comes straight after the penultimate one.

## SYMMETRICAL HEADS 2

*OBJECTIVE: TO CREATE TWO NEW SYMMETRICAL
IMAGES USING EACH SIDE OF A PHOTOGRAPH OF
SOMEONE'S FACE*

Photographs need to be as specified in Symmetrical
Heads 1 in Section 1.

### Programs and functions involved

MS Publisher or MS PowerPoint
[Ctrl] *drag*
*Crop*
*Flip* horizontally
[Alt] arrow keys (in Publisher)

[Shift] arrow keys (in PowerPoint)

**What to do**
- Load your 'donor photograph' by going to the **Insert** menu, and selecting **Picture**, followed by **From file . . . .**
- Use the *Crop* tool (it looks like XX angled upwards) to reduce the picture to a rectangle containing just the face plus a bit of unavoidable background.
- Make two exact copies of the cropped picture using [Ctrl] *drag*.
- *Crop* the copies so that one shows just the left-hand half of the face and the other just the right side. The original is to be left be unchanged as the 'Before' picture. Switch off the *Crop* tool.
- Take one cropped half and [Ctrl] *drag* a copy.
- *Flip* the copy horizontally. In Publisher, go to the **Arrange** menu and choose **Rotate** or **Flip** followed by **Flip horizontal**. In PowerPoint, click on **Draw** (on the Drawing toolbar) and choose **Rotate** or **Flip** followed by **Flip horizontal**.
- Join the two halves together and align them using [Alt] with the arrow keys in Publisher and [Shift] with the arrow keys in PowerPoint.
- Do the same with the other cropped half of the face and position the two new 'faces' alongside the unaltered copy of the original face.
- Save and/or print out as you wish.

**Variations**
- Experiment with faces that are not completely square on to the camera.
- Try faces that are tilted slightly to one side.

# HYBRID VEHICLES

*OBJECTIVE: TO IMPORT TWO VEHICLE CLIPARTS AND CREATE TWO 'HYBRIDS'*

For this activity you need to have suitable cliparts ready. You have the choice of standard Windows ones, but you are better off either using a trusted clipart disk or download the result from an internet image search. Find cliparts which show vehicles side on, not angled. Ideal images also have pure colours rather than composite colours – zoom in to check. Pure colours behave better when using the *Pick color* and *Fill with color* tools.

### Programs and functions involved
MS Publisher or MS PowerPoint
*Insert picture*
*Crop*
[Ctrl] [C] and [Ctrl] [V]
Windows Paint
*Pick color*
*Fill with color*

### What to do
- Open Publisher or PowerPoint and insert your two cliparts by going to the **Insert** menu, choosing **Picture** and then either **Clip art . . .** or **From file**. You may need to flip one of the cliparts.
- Use the *Crop* tool (it looks like XX angled upwards) to remove the front of one vehicle and the rear of the other. Then switch off *Crop*.
- Move the two remaining halves together and compare the cut edges. Resize one or both so that the edges to be joined are the same size.
- Take one half vehicle at a time and use [Ctrl] [C] and [Ctrl] [V] to paste them into Windows Paint, and put the two halves together.
- Choose which vehicle's colour(s) you want to use

and select by clicking the *Pick color* tool on that part of the vehicle. Use *Fill with color* and possibly *Brush* to apply the colour scheme of one half onto the other.

- *Select* the 'new' vehicle and save it using **Copy to...** from the **Edit** menu, or paste it back into your original program.
- Return to Publisher or PowerPoint, select *Crop* and restore the cropped half of each clipart by pulling back on the crop handles.
- Now crop off the other halves of the vehicles and repeat the process above to produce a second 'new' vehicle.

**Variations**
- Use two different vehicle types: car and motorbike, car and bus, etc.
- Use aircraft with another aircraft or vehicle.

## HYBRID CREATURES

*OBJECTIVE: TO IMPORT TWO ANIMAL CLIPARTS AND CREATE TWO 'HYBRIDS'*

As with Hybrid Vehicles you need to have suitable cliparts ready. Find cliparts which show creatures side on. Again, images with pure colours are much easier to manipulate – avoid cliparts with composite colours. Zoom in to check.

**Programs and functions involved**
MS Publisher or MS PowerPoint
*Insert picture*
Windows Paint
*Free-form select* with *Draw opaque* disabled
*Pick color*
*Fill with color*
[Ctrl] [X] and [Ctrl] [V] to *Cut* and *Paste*

**What to do**

- Open Publisher or PowerPoint and insert your two cliparts by going to the **Insert** menu, choosing **Picture** and then either **Clip art . . .** or **From file**. You may need to *flip* one of the cliparts.
- Move the images about while you decide where to join them – between front and hind legs? At the neck? You may have to resize them in order to have the planned joining edges the same length.
- Take one creature at a time and use [Ctrl] [C] and [Ctrl] [V] to paste them into Windows Paint.
- For the sake of explanation, let us suppose you are just swapping their heads over. Drag the *Free-form select* tool around the head and across the neck then use [Ctrl] [X] to *Cut* the head to the clipboard.
- Now drag *Free-form select* around the other creature's head, drag it over and attach it to the first creature's neck.
- Use [Ctrl] [V] to paste back the first head. Move it over and place it on the second creature's neck.
- Use *Pick color* to select each creature's colours and use *Fill with color* and *Brush* to colour the transplanted parts.
- Select the 'new' creatures and save them using **Copy to . . .** from the **Edit** menu.

**Variations**

- Try a variety of species and a bit of imagination.
- Mix species – how about a cat with a canary's head?

## STACKING UP

*OBJECTIVE: TO QUICKLY STACK UP 3D SHAPES (CUBOIDS OR CYLINDERS) AND RE-STACK*

**Programs and functions involved**
MS Publisher, MS PowerPoint or MS Word
**AutoShapes** or **Custom shapes** (depending upon which

software version you are using)
**Bring to front**
**Fill color**

**What to do**

- This can be done either by pupils at adjacent computers racing each other, or by having the first to achieve the task raise both hands and call out that they have finished.
- Open Publisher, PowerPoint or Word and use **Custom shapes/AutoShapes** to draw a 3D shape such as a cube, cuboid or cylinder.
- Use [Ctrl] *drag* to make a copy standing on top of the first. Continue copying upwards until you have around ten of them.
- Use **Fill color** to give each shape in the stack a different colour. In more recent versions of the software you can also number each shape.
- Use [Ctrl] *drag* to make a duplicate stack which you then re-stack. This is done first by placing the top shape down at the bottom, followed by the next. You will notice that the second shape in the new stack does not look right – you can see the top of the shape beneath. This is because objects are layered according to the order in which they were created. To fix this you must bring the second shape to the front. In Word and PowerPoint, click on **Draw** (on the Drawing toolbar) and select **Order** then **Bring to front**. In Publisher: click on **Arrange**, select **Order** (in later versions) and click on **Bring to front**.
- Now re-stack the remaining shapes, bringing each one to the front before placing it on top of the previous one.
- When someone claims to have completed, first check that the colour/number order is completely reversed and that only the top of the top shape is visible.

**Variations**
- Specify colours for the shapes.
- Try the same activity in one of the other programs.
- Use different shapes – cylinders tend to end up looking like oil drums while the cubes/cuboids look more like crates.

## COLOUR CHANGE 1

*OBJECTIVE: TO USE POWERPOINT'S RECOLOR PICTURE TOOL TO CHANGE THE COLOURS OF CLIPARTS IN OTHER APPLICATIONS*

**Programs and functions involved**
MS PowerPoint and Paint
MS Word, Publisher or Excel
**Recolor**
[Ctrl] [C] and [V]

**What to do**
- N.B. This tool does not work with some picture formats. Select the clipart you want to change and copy/paste it into PowerPoint.
- From the **Picture** toolbar select the **Recolor picture** button. In addition to being able to change each colour, you have the option of including or not including line colours when fill colours are changed.
- There is no problem with copy/pasting the changed image straight back into Publisher. However, both Word and Excel can ignore the changes that have been made. To get around this, first paste into Paint, re-select, then copy/paste into Excel or Word.

**Variations**
- Load images from other sources such as clipart disks, saved files on your computer/network and images downloaded from the internet.

# COLOUR CHANGE 2

*OBJECTIVE: TO USE POWERPOINT'S SET TRANSPARENT COLOR TOOL TO MAKE THE BACKGROUND OF AN IMAGE TRANSPARENT*

**Programs and functions involved**
MS PowerPoint and Paint
MS Word, Publisher or Excel
[Ctrl] [C] and [V]
**Set transparent color**

**What to do**
- Note 1: This tool does not work with some picture formats.
- Note 2: This is a very useful tool to use if you have to copy/paste from Windows Paint.
- Select the clipart you want to change and copy/paste it into PowerPoint.
- From the **Picture** toolbar select the **Set transparent color** button and click on the background of the image.

**Variations**
- Load images from other sources such as clipart disks, saved files on your computer/network and images downloaded from the internet.

# COLOUR CHANGE 3

*OBJECTIVE: TO USE PAINT TO CHANGE COLOURS IN THOSE IMAGES WHICH CANNOT BE CHANGED WITH POWERPOINT'S RECOLOR TOOL, AND THEN TO MAKE THE BACKGROUND TRANSPARENT*

**Programs and functions involved**
MS PowerPoint and Paint
MS Word, Publisher or Excel

[Ctrl] [C] and [V]
**Set transparent color**

**What to do**
- Select the clipart you want to change and copy/paste it into Paint.
- Select colours using the *Color box*, or *Pick color*. You can also alter a chosen colour or create your own entirely by clicking on the **Color** menu, then **Edit colors...** and selecting **Define custom color**.
- Use the *Fill with color*, *Brush* and *Pencil* tools, possibly in conjunction with the *Magnify* tool, to make the changes you wish. If an original colour is composite (i.e. made by combining pixels of different colours), the *Fill with color* tool is not effective, and the task possibly not worth the time and effort required.

**Variations**
- Load images from other sources such as clipart disks, saved files on your computer/network and images downloaded from the internet.

## ROTATING COPIES

*OBJECTIVE: TO CREATE A ROTATIONALLY SYMMETRICAL IMAGE FROM MULTIPLE COPIES OF A TRANSPARENT BACKGROUND IMAGE*

**Programs and functions involved**
MS PowerPoint
Windows Paint
**Set transparent color**

**What to do**
- Import a picture of someone into PowerPoint and crop and/or reduce its size so that its height is about a third of the page area and its width about a

quarter of its height. The picture needs to have a transparent background; if it does not, follow this procedure:

1. Load a group photograph into Paint and using *Free-form select*, copy one person onto the clipboard.
2. Paste it into PowerPoint.
3. With the pasted picture still selected, click on the **Set transparent color** icon (it's on the **Picture** toolbar) and click on the white background area of the picture.

- Use [Ctrl] *drag* to make a copy, then use the green *rotate handle* to turn the copy about 45°. Overlap the bottom of the copy with the bottom of the original.
- Repeat this copy and rotate routine, adding copies as if they are the petals of a flower. When You have finished select all the copies (by dragging the cursor around them) and group them together.

### Variations

- To make your image more flower-like, copy and rotate a smaller, darker picture to place in the centre, or simply place a face in the centre.

## CONNECTORS

*OBJECTIVE: TO MAKE AND MANIPULATE A SIMPLE FLOW CHART USING* CONNECTORS *TO LINK THE BOXES*

### Programs and functions involved
MS PowerPoint

### What to do

- Design a simple flow chart using pictures, text boxes or *AutoShapes*. (N.B. text can be added to *Autoshapes* by right-clicking on them and choosing **Add text**.) You could, for example, use pictures with text boxes to illustrate the water cycle.

- From the **AutoShapes** button (on the **Draw** toolbar), select *Connectors* and click the line or arrow style you want. Move the cursor over the first object you wish to connect – as you do so, tiny blue connector anchors appear. Click on one of these.
- Now move over the other object you are linking to and click on one of its anchors.
- With the connector in place you can alter the colour and line thickness and style of arrowheads using buttons on the **Draw** toolbar.
- Add in further connectors. When you have finished, move objects about and watch the connectors mutate in order to stay connected.

### Variations
- Edit colours of lines, autoshapes, text, text boxes, etc.
- Set the group the task of making a simple, prescribed flow chart as a race. Compare the first finished with the efforts of those who have taken more care and time over the task.

# 3D SHAPES

*OBJECTIVE: TO USE A 3D **AUTOSHAPE/CUSTOM SHAPES** TO DRAW A CUBOID AND THEN REPLICATE IT USING SEPARATE 2D **AUTOSHAPES/CUSTOM SHAPES***

### Programs and functions involved
MS PowerPoint or Publisher (You could also use MS Excel but there is little point, as you don't need a spreadsheet format)
### AutoShapes/Custom shapes
[Ctrl] [C] and [V]

**What to do**

- Depending upon which version of which program you are using, select either, from the Drawing toolbar, **AutoShapes** then **Basic shapes**, or (with older versions) click on the **Custom shapes** button.
- Choose the 3D cuboid tool and drag out a cuboid.
- Use the rectangle tool to draw an oblong the same width as the cuboid.
- Use the parallelogram tool to draw a top and side to add to the oblong. These parallelograms will have to be adapted to fit – you can resize using the corner and side handles, rotate using the green handle, and skew using the yellow handle.
- Give each of the three parts a separate fill colour and assemble them as a new cuboid. For fine, precise movements hold down [Shift] in PowerPoint, [Ctrl] in Excel, or [Alt] in Publisher and use the arrow keys.
- Fix all three components together.
  In Publisher select all three parts either by dragging around them or using [Ctrl] *click*, then click on the **Group objects** button which appears when more than one object is selected.
  In PowerPoint and Excel, click on the **Draw** button on the Drawing toolbar and select **Group**.

**Variations**

- Make other 3D shapes from 2D shapes.

# THE SQUARES GAME 2

*OBJECTIVE: TO PRACTISE SELECTING AND ALIGNING ELEMENTS WHILE PLAYING A QUICK AND SIMPLE STRATEGY GAME*

Like The Squares Game 1 in Section 1, it is based on The Matchstick Game, as featured in *Jumpstart Numeracy*.

**Programs and functions involved**

MS Publisher or MS PowerPoint (also works in MS Excel)

**Arrange/Align or distribute** (or **Align objects** in some versions)

**What to do**

- While holding down [Shift], use the rectangle tool to draw a square.
- Use [Ctrl] *drag* to make a column of two squares to the right of the first, followed by columns of three, four and five squares.
- If you wish you can colour them using a different colour for each column.
- Highlight the two squares in the second column. You can do this either by dragging around them or by using [Ctrl] *click*. Align them using **Align or distribute**, or **Align objects**, depending upon which version you have.
  In Publisher you access this through the **Arrange** menu. In PowerPoint (and Excel) you access it through the **Draw** button on the Drawing toolbar.
- Choose one of the **Left to right** options – any will do.
- Now align the squares in the columns of 3, 4 and 5.
- If you wish to be pernickety, you can also align horizontally the squares in the odd-numbered columns and the squares in the even-numbered columns.
- Select all 15 squares and copy them to the clipboard. You might also want to save it as a file for future use.
- To play the game there are only two rules:
  Rule 1: When it's your turn you may delete as many squares as you like that are the same colour (i.e. in the same column).
  Rule 2: The winner is the player who leaves the other player the last square.
- While playing the game a number of winning

patterns will become apparent, such as leaving your opponent two pairs of squares.

**Variations**
- Use different shapes/autoshapes instead of squares.
- Arrange a knockout competition.

# DESIGN A PLAYING CARD

*OBJECTIVE: TO ASSEMBLE AN IMAGE OF A (NON-ROYAL) PLAYING CARD AND LOCK ALL ELEMENTS TOGETHER*

**Programs and functions involved**
MS Publisher or MS PowerPoint
**Arrange/Align or distribute** (or **Align objects** in some versions)/**Left to right**
*Text boxes*
Windows *Character Map*

**What to do**
- Use the rectangle tool to draw an oblong which will form the boundary of the playing card. Check that the fill colour is white, not transparent.
- Open up Windows *Character Map* and search for the card suit symbol of your choice (diamond, heart, club or spade). If your chosen font does not have these symbols use the Symbol font.
- Select the symbol (either by double-clicking or using the **Select** button), then click **Copy**.
- Drag out a small *text box* (approx. 1–2 cm square) and paste the symbol in. In some program versions you may have to reset the font selected to the same as in the *Character Map*.
- [Ctrl] *drag* a few copies of the *text box* and add the appropriate numeral to two of them.
- Arrange the text boxes on the card, remembering the convention of inverting the lower symbols and

numeral. Do this by rotating with the green *rotate handle*. You can align them (as described in Squares Game 2).

- Select all the objects by dragging around them and group them together (as described in 3D Shapes).

**Variations**
- Select the completed card, paste a copy into Windows Paint and use **Edit, Copy to...** to save it as a separate image.
- Commission different students to do different cards (to an agreed size) and save them as separate images.

## CAPTURE A CARD SUIT

*OBJECTIVE: TO ASSEMBLE A SUIT OF 13 CARDS WITH IMAGES CAPTURED AND CROPPED FROM A GAME. THE FIRST STUDENT TO GET A WHOLE SUIT IS THE WINNER*

**Programs and functions involved**
MS Publisher or MS PowerPoint
Windows Paint
A computer card game such as FreeCell or Solitaire
[Print Screen] key

**What to do**
- Open Publisher or PowerPoint, Paint and your chosen card game.
- Start the game and press the [Print Screen] key to copy the image to the *clipboard*.
- Decide which suit you have most of – this is the suit you are going to collect.
- Switch to Paint and paste in the screen image.
- Press the [Escape] key then use *select* to highlight a card. Copy it to the clipboard, then paste it into Publisher or PowerPoint.

- Return to Paint to get copies of non-duplicates of the same suit. Arrange them in order, leaving space for missing members of the suit. Make a note of which cards you still need to capture.
- Return to the game and play it until another 'wanted' card appears. Repeat the [Print Screen] paste into Paint and copy routine and continue till you have a full set.

**Variations**
- When you select individual cards use **Edit, Copy to...** to save them as separate images.
- Commission different students to do different suits and save them as separate images, building up a full deck between you.

## CARD SHUFFLE

*OBJECTIVE: TO SHUFFLE CARDS STACKED ONE ON TOP OF THE OTHER*

**Programs and functions involved**
MS Publisher or MS PowerPoint

**What to do**
- For this activity you need to insert a number of playing cards, either a suit made and saved from Capture a Card Suit or Design a Playing Card.
- The order of insertion determines how the cards are stacked. As you insert them lay them out, overlapping.
- Select all the cards by dragging around them. Align them centrally, both horizontally and vertically. Precise alignment expressions vary according to which software version you use.
- Shuffle cards around using: **Bring to front, Bring forward, Send to back,** and **Send backward.** In Publisher these are in the **Arrange** menu. In

PowerPoint, click on **Draw** on the Drawing toolbar, then click on **Order**.
- Set a task such as arranging specific cards (e.g. the 3, 4, 5 and 6) in the correct order, so that each overlaps the previous value card.

### Variations
- Ask for a gin rummy hand, a running flush, etc.
- Ask for the cards to be overlapped in reverse order.

## WHO'S THE CELEB?

*OBJECTIVE: TO MAKE A 'WHO'S THE CELEBRITY?'-TYPE PUZZLE USING A GRID OF OPAQUE TEXT BOXES TO OBSCURE A PHOTOGRAPH*

### Programs and functions involved
Internet image search
MS Publisher
*Text boxes*
**Arrange/Align or distribute** (or **Align objects** in some versions)

### What to do
- Find a suitable photograph of a 'celebrity'. Using an 'advanced' image search option on one of the main search engines will be quicker as it allows you to search by full name (as a phrase), size (you only want medium or large images), colour and file type (you want a JPG/JPEG).
  Ideally you want a photograph that is mostly face, unless you want to leave clues (e.g. microphone, football strip, etc.).
- Adjust the size of the image so that its width and height are convenient for dividing into an equal number of rectangles. For the purpose of illustration, suppose you have sized a photograph which is 12 cm wide and 18 cm tall.

- As 12 cm is divisible by 3, and 18 cm is divisible by 3, make a text box 4 cm (12 cm ÷ 3) wide and 6 cm (18 cm ÷ 3) deep. Type in a number 1 (about size 36) and centre it. Give the text box a coloured background.
- For this example you will need six rows of three text boxes to obscure the photograph. Make your first row of three by [Ctrl] *dragging* two more text boxes and placing them side by side. If necessary use **Arrange/Align or distribute** to line them up horizontally.
- Select all the text boxes in this row and use [Ctrl] *drag* to add further rows – for this example another five. Again, you can use **Arrange/Align or distribute** to keep it tidy.
- Edit the text boxes by numbering them.
- Remember to save the file. To play the game, people select a numbered text box and delete it.

### Variations
- Save files and swap them – how many boxes do you have to remove before you can identify the face?
- Save the grid of text boxes and use them with another photograph, sized to fit beneath them.

## JIGLESS PUZZLES

*OBJECTIVE: TO SPLIT A PICTURE INTO RECTANGULAR PIECES WHICH CAN THEN BE REASSEMBLED BY SOMEONE ELSE*

**Programs and functions involved**
Internet image search
MS Publisher
Rulers
*Crop*

**What to do**

- Find a suitable photograph, possibly from the internet, and resize it so that its height and width are multiples of 5 cm.
- Move the vertical ruler across and align the zero with the top left-hand corner of the photograph.
- Select the *Crop* tool; position the cursor over the handle in the centre of the bottom edge of the picture and crop off all the way up until you reach 5 cm on the ruler.
- [Ctrl] *drag* a copy of this over to the side of the screen.
- Now re-select the cropped picture, re-activate crop, return to the centre-bottom handle and move it down to the 10 cm mark on the ruler.
- Now position the *Crop* cursor over the centre-top handle and crop down to the 5 cm mark.
- [Ctrl] *drag* a copy of this to the side, return to the cropped image, restore another 5 cm from the bottom and cut off another 5 cm from the top. Continue until the whole of the picture is in strips at the side.
- Move the first strip back to the centre and align its top-left corner with the zero on the horizontal ruler. Use *Crop* on the centre-right handle to cut off all but the first 5 cm, then drag a copy over to the opposite side.
- Crop the rest of the row into 5 cm pieces, placing them on top of each other at the side.
- Do the same with the other strips, stacking the pieces of each strip in a separate pile.
- Challenge a partner to assemble your puzzle faster than you can assemble theirs.

**Variations**

- Save files and swap them – how many boxes do you have to remove before you can identify the face?
- Use oblong pieces.
- If the puzzle has few pieces, allow the puzzle maker to rotate them.

## COMPOSITE PICTURES

*OBJECTIVE: TO COMPOSE A SCENE MADE UP OF SEPARATE IMPORTED IMAGES*

**Programs and functions involved**
Internet image search
MS Publisher or Paintbrush
Optional additional use of Windows Paint
A good selection of clipart images, ideally from CD-ROM disc collections

**What to do**
- Select cliparts which can be used to make up a scene, e.g. a building such as a house, perhaps a car to park outside, a couple of trees and people, and perhaps pets.
- Arrange the separate pictures using size, and position up the page to give perspective.
- Some of the pictures may need to be brought forward or sent backwards using the **Order** options from the **Draw** menu.
- You can use the line tool to add perspective and detail, e.g. by drawing a driveway for the car.
- Some of the cliparts can have their colours adjusted using PowerPoint's **Recolor picture** tool. These can also be edited by pasting them into Windows Paint and pasting them back again.
- Parts of the cliparts can be erased using 'electronic tippex' – white-filled shapes with no line (use the **Line color** drop-down options) placed over the top. Use [Shift] with the arrow keys to adjust the position.

**Variations**
- Use a graduated, coloured background. From the **Format** menu choose **Background**, drop down the arrow by the colour pane, choose **Fill effects**, then either one of the presets or create your own using

two colours. The **Horizontal shading styles** are more suitable.

## SYMMETRICAL LANDSCAPES

*OBJECTIVE: TO USE A PHOTOGRAPH OF A LANDSCAPE TO PRODUCE AN IMAGE WITH VERTICAL AND HORIZONTAL SYMMETRY*

**Programs and functions involved**
Internet image search
MS PowerPoint or MS Publisher

**What to do**
- Find a landscape photograph from a file or from an internet image search. Good pictures to use are ones which feature mountains and therefore do not have a horizontal interface between ground and sky.
- Make a copy of the picture and flip it horizontally.
- Align the two copies and join them together – use [Shift] arrow keys (PowerPoint) or [Alt] arrow keys (Publisher) to make fine adjustments. In Publisher it also helps to hide the boundaries and guides either through the **View** menu or by using the [Ctrl]+[Shift]+[O] shortcut.
- Group these two copies together and make a copy below. Flip this copy and align and join beneath. Group all four components together.

**Variations**
- Make one copy of the original and rotate it 180° before aligning and joining to the bottom of the original.
- Start with two copies of the original picture and crop off the left and right halves. Take one half-picture and make a copy which you then flip over and join on to the non-flipped half. Repeat with the other half-picture.

- Try rotating the original 180° and placing it on top of the copy.

## DESIGN A ROOM

*OBJECTIVE: TO MAKE A SCALE DRAWING OF AN IMAGINARY 4-METRE BY 3-METRE BEDROOM AND ARRANGE FURNITURE IN IT*

**Programs and functions involved**
MS Publisher

**What to do**
- For simplicity, use a 1:20 scale. This means that all you have to do is to divide 'real' dimensions by 10, then halve them (i.e. 4 m = 400 cm ÷ 10 = 40 cm; 40 cm halved = 20 cm).
- To begin, draw out a portrait rectangle. Using the *handle* in the centre of the bottom edge, adjust the length to 20 cm (the dimensions are displayed at the bottom-right corner of the screen). Now use the *handle* in the centre of one of the sides to set the width to 15 cm. Resizing accurately is easier if you increase the screen magnification.
- Use thick lines parallel with walls to indicate the position of a window and radiator. While holding down [Shift], draw a thick, 3·8 cm line to represent a 76 cm wide door. [Ctrl] *drag* a copy of the door line, rotate it and position it to show the door position when open. Select the entire room (walls, door and radiator) and *group* the parts together.
- For ease, draw all the furniture outside of the room boundary. This avoids accidentally selecting the room rectangle while grouping furniture parts together. Draw a bed that is 200 cm by 100 cm (scale size 10 cm x 50 cm) and colour it using *Fill with color* tool. Add a pillow at one end of the bed using the rounded rectangle autoshape and colour

it differently. Select bed and pillow together and *group* them. You may want to superimpose a *text box* label on the bed and include that in the group.

- Draw a wardrobe 120 cm by 50 cm (scale size 6 cm × 2·5 cm). To make doors for it, draw a horizontal line 3 cm long, copy it, then rotate both lines and place them at the front corners of the rectangle. Label it with a *text box* and, again, *group* together.
- Draw a chest of drawers 90 cm wide and 60 cm deep (4·5 cm × 3 cm), but add a 4·5 cm × 2·5 cm rectangle to the front to represent the space needed to pull out the drawers. Label and *group* together.
- You can now place the furniture in the room, rotating as necessary and paying attention to not blocking the door or radiator and not putting the wardrobe in front of the window.

### Variations
- Add other items of furniture: chair, desk, TV on stand, etc.

## DRAW A ROOM

*OBJECTIVE: TO MAKE A SCALE DRAWING OF A REAL ROOM AND ITS CONTENTS*

**Programs and functions involved**
MS Publisher

### What to do
- You can use the room you are in – remember your tape measure! Alternatively, have the students bring in dimensions of their own bedrooms as a well-planned piece of homework.
- Choose an appropriate scale; for a classroom/IT suite a scale of 1:100 would be most appropriate. For real bedrooms stick to 1:20 as in Design a Room.

- With a real room you need to position fixed items such as doors, windows and radiators in the correct location. To mark distances along walls on your scale drawing, use temporary lines of the appropriate length in a different colour. You can delete them after positioning a fixture. With a 1:100 scale a distance of 1 m will require a line 1 cm long compared to 5 cm long on a 1:20 scale.
- Group the walls together with fixed items such as doors, worktops, windows, etc.
- Make your moveable items outside the boundary of the room, then move them in when you're ready. If you must show 20 or 30 IT suite swivel chairs, represent each as a circle of appropriate diameter to include leg room beyond the chair itself.

### Variations
- Use the plan to test out alternative layouts. Measure plan distances with temporary lines and scale them up to real size.

## DESIGN A POSTER AND FLYER

*OBJECTIVE: TO DESIGN AN A4-SIZED POSTER TO GIVE SPECIFIC INFORMATION AND THEN ADAPT IT TO MAKE A PAIR OF A5-SIZED FLYERS*

### Programs and functions involved
MS Publisher

### What to do
- Open Publisher and insert a second page. From the **Arrange** menu select **Layout guides** and set all margins to 1 cm. Leave columns as 1 but change rows to 2.
- Give a specification for what information needs to be included: event, date, time, venue, cost, where to buy tickets, etc. Discuss the variety of styles that

might be suitable for the type of event. Specify that it must contain at least one wordart and one relevant picture.

- While pupils are busy designing, several issues may arise:
  - Do text boxes have colour, including white, or 'no fill', i.e. transparent?
  - Order – as each object is added it is layered above the last, so where one overlaps another it may be necessary to change the order (as described in Stacking Up) to avoid blocking out an object created earlier.
  - Does the poster look balanced? Are there lots of boxes on one side?
  - Do objects need to be aligned? (See Shape Race 2 for how to do this in Publisher.)
- When the poster has been OK'd, select all the objects and group them together (as described in 3D Shapes). Copy to the clipboard and paste onto the second page of the file.
- On the second page rotate the group 90° and use a corner *handle* to reduce the group in size until it fits entirely above or below the horizontal centre layout guide.
- Return the group to vertical and check it over, particularly text boxes where the text may have to be made smaller to fit. Ungroup if necessary to make adjustments and to add or delete information needed or not needed on the flyer compared to the poster, e.g. 'Bring this flyer with you to admit a second person for half price'.
- Group all the objects again, rotate 90° again and use [Ctrl] *drag* to make a second copy on the other side of the centre layout guide.

### Variations
- Make a monochrome version of the poster and flyer which would be more suitable for use on a monochrome photocopier.

# ANIMATION 1

*OBJECTIVE: TO ANIMATE THE ENTRANCE AND EXIT OF A CLIPART IMAGE*

**Programs and functions involved**
MS PowerPoint
**Custom animation**

**What to do**
- For this you need a suitable clipart:
  - something that is meant to move, e.g. a vehicle, aircraft or boat;
  - ideally a full side view;
  - no background or shadow.
- When you have inserted the clipart adjust its size so that its length is no bigger than approximately one fifth of the page width.
- Right-click it and choose **Custom animation**. Click down the **Add effect** list and choose **Entrance**. Try the **Fly in** option and select the **Direction** and **Speed**.
- Click on **Add effect** again choose **Exit**. Try the **Fly out** option and set the appropriate **Direction** and **Speed**.
- To play the slideshow animation, either use [Shift] [F5] or click the slideshow button. The default start is to click the mouse, but you can change subsequent effects to follow on after the previous ones.

**Variations**
- Instead of using separate entrance and exit effects choose **Motion paths**. The basic ones are self-explanatory. When one has been selected you can click on the marked path and adjust its start and end points by dragging on the green and red arrow heads. You may now want to position the clipart just off the page.
- You may want to try **Draw custom path/Scribble** which allows you to draw the route which the clipart will take.

- Insert a background photograph – you'll need to go to the **Draw** menu, select **Order** and click on **Send to back**.

## ANIMATION 2

*OBJECTIVE: TO ANIMATE THE ENTRANCE, EXIT AND RETURN OF A CLIPART IMAGE*

**Programs and functions involved**
MS PowerPoint
**Custom animation**

**What to do**
- For this you need a suitable clipart as described for Animation 1 and positioned just off the page ready to make its entrance.
- When you have adjusted the clipart's size, [Ctrl] *drag* a copy of it over to the other side of the work area and *flip* it over horizontally, ready for its return. Place this copy slightly higher up the page and reduce its size slightly in order to get a sense of perspective.
- Select the first copy of the image, right-click on it and choose **Custom animation**. Select **Add effect** list and choose **Entrance**. Choose the **Fly in** or **Crawl in** option and set the **Direction** and **Speed**.
- Click on **Add effect** again choose **Exit**. Choose **Fly out** or **Crawl out** and set the appropriate **Direction** and **Speed**.
- With the exit animation selected in the custom animation window, drop down the **Start:** options box and select **After previous**.
- Right-click on the flipped copy of the image and add entrance and exit effects as described above. Change the **Start:** option for the entrance and exit to **After previous**.
- The panel in the **Custom animation** window should

now show the two entrances and two exits in the order in which they should occur. Right-click on the second entrance instruction and select **Timing....** Set a time delay of a couple of seconds to give the impression that the first image has gone out of sight and turned around before returning across the page.

- Play the slideshow animation either using [Shift] [F5] or the slideshow button.

### Variations

- Use a faster speed for the exit than for the entrance; this will give the impression of acceleration.
- Replace the entrance and exit effects with **Motion paths** as described in Animation 1.
- Replace the entrance and exit effects with freehand drawn paths using **Draw custom path/Scribble**, remembering to start and finish off the edge of the paper.
- Insert a background photograph as described in Animation 1.

## ANIMATION 3

*OBJECTIVE: TO PRODUCE AN ANIMATED 'STORY' USING CLIPART IMAGES*

**Programs and functions involved**
MS PowerPoint
**Custom animation**

**What to do**

- For this you need several suitable cliparts as described for Animation 1. If you wish you can also use a photograph or picture instead of a background.
- *Either*: insert the image you've chosen as a background; *or*: from the **Format** menu choose **Background**, drop down the arrow on the colour window, select **Fill effects...** and create a landscape

effect using two colours and a horizontal style.

- Take each clipart in turn, position it where you want it to start and animate its movements as outlined in Animation 1. You may wish to have some of the cliparts begin on the page or remain on the page after their movements.
- Set the **Start:** of each animation to begin **After previous** and use a time delay between movements, as described in Animation 2.
- Play the slideshow animation either using [Shift] [F5] or the slideshow button. If it doesn't look right, make adjustments to the position of the images, their motion paths, speeds and directions.

**Variations**

- Change the order of the movements using the **Re-order** arrows on the **Custom animation** window.
- Choose different entrance and exit effects.
- Add sounds to the movements as described in Animation Sound.

## ANIMATION SOUND

*OBJECTIVE: TO IMPORT SOUNDS INTO AN ANIMATION SEQUENCE*

**Programs and functions involved**
MS PowerPoint
**Insert Sound from file**

**What to do**

- For this you need to begin with a PowerPoint file containing an animation sequence as described in the three previous activities.
- You need a saved sound file. The easiest option is to use one of the many websites which have sound effect files for download. An advanced search using 'sound effects' as a phrase plus 'free download' in

the 'containing all the words' box should give you plenty of sites to peruse. Other options include using a sound effects CD or a microphone.

- Determine how long you need the sound to last. Open the sound file in Windows **Sound recorder**. This displays the total length of the sound and, while playing or paused, the length of sound already elapsed.
- If the sound is too long, play it through a couple of times and pause it where you want it to start. From the **Edit** menu choose **Delete before current position**. Similarly, pause where you want the sound to stop and **Delete after current position**.
- The pitch of the sound can be altered by changing the speed. You can also alter it by changing its volume and direction and by adding echo. Remember to save the file under a new name.
- Return to PowerPoint, and from the **Insert** menu choose **Movies and sounds** and select **Sound from file**. Select the saved file, and when asked, choose to start the sound in the slide show **Automatically**.
- Move the speaker icon off the page, placing it, for convenience, next to the image you've assigned it to.
- If necessary, re-order the sound in the **Custom animation** window so that it is immediately below the movement it applies to. Click on the 'media' label and alter the **Start:** to **With previous**.
- You may well have to use trial and error to fine tune matching the sound to the movement. It may be necessary to right-click on either the movement or the media label and choose the **Timing** option to insert a delay.

**Variations**
- Edit the sounds used using other options in Windows Sound Recorder.

## TRIPLE SNAP

*OBJECTIVE: TO USE RANDOM NUMBER GENERATION AND THE **IF** FUNCTION TO CREATE A NUMERIC VERSION OF A 'FRUIT MACHINE' WHICH CHANGES EACH TIME THE [F9] KEY IS PRESSED*

**Programs and functions involved**
MS Excel
**=RANDBETWEEN**(<value>,<value>)

**What to do**
- In cells A1, D1 and G1 insert: **=RANDBETWEEN(1,5)**. Note: To use the RANDBETWEEN function you must have the **Analysis Toolpak** enabled. To do this go to the **Tools** menu and click on **Add-Ins . . . .**
- Increase font size to around 72, put a border around them and/or give them differently coloured backgrounds.
- Each time the [F9] key is pressed a new set of random numbers appear. The task is to count how many presses of [F9] it takes before the same number appears in each cell.
- When some, or most, pupils have stopped on three identical numerals (and you have checked that they haven't simply typed the numerals in), see who took fewest and most presses.
- Change all three cells to **=RANDBETWEEN(1,6)** and invite predictions as to how many presses it will take now. Test it out.
- Try out just two random number cells but with a greater range, e.g. **=RANDBETWEEN(1,20)** cells.
- A lot of cheap combination locks have three tumblers with ten numerals. Set up three random number cells **=RANDBETWEEN(0,9)** and see how many goes it takes before a predetermined code is displayed. This requires the numerals to be displayed in the same order.

### Variations

- Vary the number of random number cells and the range of each.
- Use cells with different ranges, e.g. (1,4) and (1,10).
- Make a lottery number simulation machine using six random cells. To allow for there being one ball less each time one is drawn use the following in your six cells: =**RANDBETWEEN(1,49)**, =**RANDBETWEEN(1,48)**, =**RANDBETWEEN(1,47)**, =**RANDBETWEEN(1,46)**, =**RANDBETWEEN(1,45)**, and =**RANDBETWEEN(1,44)**.
  There is, of course, a likelihood of duplicates, so if you wish, add an extra cell to substitute for a duplicated number. Use =**RANDBETWEEN(1,47)** on the basis that at least two numbers have been drawn.

## KEY WORDS

*OBJECTIVE: TO USE **AUTOSHAPES** WITH LETTERS TO SIMULATE LETTER KEYS AND USE THEM TO WRITE WORDS OR PHRASES*

This can either be a challenge against the clock to do one's own name or else a race for everyone to do the same phrase or sentence.

### Programs and functions involved
MS PowerPoint
**AutoShape**

### What to do
- From the **AutoShapes** menu (on the Drawing toolbar), select **Basic shapes** then the 3D shape which resembles a keyboard button. Use it to drag out a representation of one of the letter keys.
- Right-click on this shape, choose the **Add** text option and type a capital letter onto it. Adjust the font and size to fit.

- Now use [Ctrl] *drag* to make copies and align them horizontally. (**Draw** menu/**Align or distribute/Align top**).
- Right-clicking on a copy gives you the option to **Edit text**. Use this to change letters to make up words or phrases. Tidy up the appearance by moving the shapes sideways only, by holding down [Shift] while pressing the horizontal arrow keys.

### Variations

- Do not allow a letter to be used more than once.
- Specify the size of the letter keys by setting the dimensions of your first autoshape: highlight it, select **AutoShape** from the **Format** menu, then select the **size** tab. The others will then be the same size when you [Ctrl] *drag* copies.
- Wait until all the 'letter keys' have been made, highlight them all and set the size (as above).

## MULTIPLICATION CHART GENERATOR

*OBJECTIVE: TO MAKE A SPREADSHEET WHICH GENERATES TIMES TABLE CHARTS BY THE INSERTION OF A NUMBER, USING AN ABSOLUTE REFERENCE IN AN EXCEL SPREADSHEET TO AVOID HAVING TO EDIT RELATIVE REFERENCES*

### Programs and functions involved
MS Excel
*Absolute references*

### What to do

- Give cell A1 a background colour and type in a number (e.g. 2) to determine which times table is to be generated.
- Put a 1 into A4 and x in B4.
- In C4 put the *absolute reference* =$A$1.

69

- In D4 insert a space followed by the equals symbol (=). You must start with a space to prevent the cell from expecting a formula to follow.
- In E4 insert the formula =A4*C4.
- Highlight the row and centrally format the cells.
- Select cells A4 to E4, hold the cursor over the *fill handle* in the bottom right of E4 and drag downwards. Stop at row 13 if you want a tables chart up to 10 x. Carry on downwards if you want lots more.
- To change the chart to another times table simply insert a new number in A1.

**Variations**
- Smarten the table up by altering font, font size, colour, cell background, etc.
- Identify the sequence pattern of the units in column E.
- See who can be first to create four specified tables charts and copy/paste them into a Word file.
- How big a number do you need in cell A1 before the lower part of column E becomes too narrow to fit the values?

## ESCALATING NUMBERS

*OBJECTIVE: TO MAKE A SPREADSHEET WHICH DEMONSTRATES HOW NUMBERS CAN ESCALATE THROUGH REPEATED MULTIPLICATION, USING RELATIVE REFERENCES IN AN EXCEL SPREADSHEET*

**Programs and functions involved**
MS Excel
*Relative references*

**What to do**

Doubling

- Put a 1 into A1.
- In A2 put the formula =a1*2.
- Select cell A2, hold the cursor over the *fill handle* in the bottom-right corner and drag downwards. Each cell will be double the value of the cell above. How many rows can you drag down before the cells become ######ed?
  Widen the columns to get rid of the ######. With very large numbers you will need to reformat the column: go to the **Format** menu, select **Cells...**, click on **Number** and set it to **0** decimal places. Also, tick the box to use the **1000 separator**. You will, however, still arrive at a point where you cannot make the columns wide enough.
- Try again in other columns but using *3 and *4 in the formulae.

Squaring

- Put a 2 into (for example) cell E1. In E2 put the formula =E1*E1.
- Select cell E2 and drag downwards on the *fill handle*, as far as row 6 or 7. Each cell will be the square of the previous cell. The increase in value will be such that cells will become #####ed very quickly.

**Variations**

- Try a cubing column using the formula = F1*F1*F1 – you should be able to reach row four before being ######ed.

# LISTING

*OBJECTIVE: TO EXPLORE AND CREATE CUSTOM LISTS IN EXCEL SPREADSHEET*

**Programs and functions involved**
MS Excel
*Custom lists*

**What to do**
Simple word lists
- Select a cell and type in the name of a month, either as a whole word or in its abbreviated form. Drag on the *fill handle* and subsequent months should fill in automatically. If they do not, you may have to add them to the *Custom lists* (see below).
- Try starting with a day or its abbreviated form.

Make your own custom list
- You may wish to create a *custom list* using names of students in your group, class names, premiership football clubs, etc. There are two ways to do this:
1. From the **Tools** menu choose **Options...** and select the **Custom lists** tab. With NEW LIST displayed in the custom lists box, type your words into the **List entries** box on the right, then click on the **Add** button followed by **OK.**
2. Type your new list of words into a range of cells and highlight them before going to the **Custom lists** tab. On the **Custom lists** tab the highlighted cells should be displayed in the **Import list from cells** box as *Absolute references*. Click on the **Import** button and then **OK.**

Listing numbers with steps
- Put two number values into adjoining cells (vertically or horizontally) and highlight them. Drag down (or across) and the cells will be filled sequentially using the same 'step' value. If you

entered two consecutive integers, such as 1 and 2 (known as a 'step' of 1), then the cells will continue: 3, 4, 5, etc. Your 'step' value can include decimals and values larger than 1, e.g. starting with 0.25 and 0.5 will increase cells by 0.25 each time; while starting with 1 and 3 will give odd numbers. You can use use this technique to produce long lists of multiples – for example starting with 0 and 16 will produce your 16 times table.

Listing words with steps
- Put 'Mon' and 'Wed' into two cells, highlight them and drag on the *fill handle*. Alternate days should be omitted. Try with months using 'January' and 'April'.

Listing words with times
- Put a time (in hh:mm format) in a cell and drag on the *fill handle*. The subsequent times should be one hour after the previous.
- Put two times (with an interval between) into two adjacent cells, then highlight both and drag on the *fill handle*. This is a useful trick if you are planning appointment times at regular intervals.

**Variations**
- Drag on the *fill handle* upwards instead of downwards.

# PLAYING WITH TIME

*OBJECTIVE: TO USE THE TIME FORMAT IN EXCEL TO ADD UP AMOUNTS OF TIME AND CALCULATE TIME INTERVALS*

**Programs and functions involved**
MS Excel
hh:mm cell format
[hh]:mm cell format

**What to do**

Calculating with amounts of time

- In a column list the hours worked for each day of the week.
- Select the cell beneath the list and use the *AutoSum* button to add them up. Assuming that the total should be more than 24 hours, the result will appear to be incorrect. This is because Excel likes to exchange 24 hours for a day, though it does not automatically give you days, hours and minutes.
- To correct this formatting glitch, highlight your 'Total Time' cell and click on **Cells...** on the **Format** menu. Choose **Custom**, and in the **Type:** box, enter [hh]:mm. The square brackets prevent the hours from being converted to days when the total reaches 24 hours.
- Using this format you can add, subtract, multiply and divide periods of time.

Calculating time intervals

- Using 24-hour clock format, you can calculate a time interval, such as the duration of a train journey, by subtracting the start time from the finish time. If the start time is on a previous day, it will be necessary to add 24 to the hours of the finish time.

**Variations**

- Multiply an amount of time, e.g. the duration of an IT lesson by the numer of lessons.
- Divide an amount of time, e.g. the length of a lesson by the number of pupils.

# INVOICE GENERATOR

*OBJECTIVE: TO MAKE A SPREADSHEET TO CREATE SIMPLE INVOICES*

**Programs and functions involved**
MS Excel
*Relative references*
*Absolute references*
*AutoSum*

**What to do**

- Below is an example which can be adapted to suite your requirements. The top two rows have been left blank to allow a title and address to go in.
- Label column headings as follows: in A5: **Item**; in B5: **Quantity**; in C5: **Unit price**; in D5: **Cost**; in E5: **VAT**; and in F5: **Cost incl. VAT**. Put bold borders around these title cells.
- In E3 put **VAT at:** and justify the cell to the right. In F3 put **17.5%** and justify left.
- Insert the following formulae in the following cells: in D6: **=B6*C6**; in E5: **=D6*$F$3**; and in F5 either: **=SUM(D6:E6)** or: **=D6+E6**.
- Now select cells B6 to F6 and drag the *fill handle* down to include row 15. Because you've used an *absolute reference* in E5 it remains unchanged while the other references are adjusted when you fill down.
- Highlight the six columns down to row 15 and give them borders.
- Select D17, click on the *AutoSum* button and drag down from D6 to D15, inserting the range of cells to be totalled. Use E18 to total the VAT levied and F19 for the total cost including VAT.
- Label the totals as follows, justifying the cells to the right: in C17: **Total excluding VAT**; in D18: **Total VAT**; and in E19: **Total including VAT**.
- Make rows 17 to 19 deeper by dragging between the grey row numbers on the right.

- Before using the invoice generator save a clean copy.

**Variations**
- Add titles, etc. to the top.
- Exclude the VAT column.
- Instead of one rate of VAT displayed in F3, insert a column between columns D and E with the heading: '**VAT at**'. When inserting the rate of VAT remember to include the % sign. Change the formula in the 'VAT' column to: =**D6\*E6**.

# ADDRESS LABEL GENERATOR 1

*OBJECTIVE: TO MAKE A SPREADSHEET WHICH REPLICATES THE CONTENTS OF AN ADDRESS LABEL INTO THE REST OF THE LABEL BOXES ON THE SHEET*

**Programs and functions involved**
MS Excel
*Absolute references*

**What to do**
- It may be necessary to adjust widths given in the following instructions to match your printer's capabilities and the size of any self-adhesive label sheets you may choose to use with this file.
- In Excel, set your left and right print margins to 0·9 (select **Page setup** from the **File** menu).
- Holding down [Ctrl], select columns A, C, E and G by clicking on them, and widen the column width to about 160 pixels. Reduce the width of columns B, D and F to about 15 pixels.
- Put a name in cell A1 and use the next four cells for lines of the address, ending with a postcode in A5. If necessary leave A4 empty.
- With cells A1 to A5 highlighted [Ctrl] *drag* a copy across into column C.

- In cell C1 insert the *absolute reference* =**$A$1**.
- Use the drag handle to copy this down into cells C2 to C5. Select each of these cells in turn and on the formula bar replace the 1 at the end of the reference for 2, 3, 4, and 5.
- Highlight cells A1 to A5, and if you wish, put a border around the label. With the entire column C label highlighted [Ctrl] *drag* copies into the top of columns E and G, then into columns A, C, E and G leaving row 6 empty so that it serves as a 'spacer' row beneath the first row of labels.
- Highlight the second row of labels and [Ctrl] *drag* further rows, leaving spacer rows.
- Make any necessary adjustments to the widths of labels and spacer columns and rows.
- To protect the formulae, highlight cells A1 to A5 then from the **Format** menu select **Cells . . .**, and on the **Protection** tab remove the tick in the **Locked** box. Now go to the **Tools** menu and select **Protection** followed by **Protect sheet**. If you wish you can remove the tick from the **Select locked cells** box. This restricts the selection of cells to just A1 to A5. Don't bother with password protection – it's hardly a confidential file!
- Now change the contents of cells A1 to A5 and all the other labels will change to match.

**Variations**
- Personalise the labels by changing font, size, etc. of the first label before copying across to column C.
- Hold a sheet of self-adhesive labels to the light with a printout of your sheet behind to see if the addresses line up with the self-adhesive labels. If they don't match (which is quite likely), adjust columns and rows until they do.

## ADDRESS LABEL GENERATOR 2

*OBJECTIVE: TO USE LINKED SPREADSHEETS IN A WORKBOOK TO MAKE A MORE REFINED VERSION OF ADDRESS LABEL GENERATOR 1*

**Programs and functions involved**
MS Excel
*Absolute references*
Cell references from one sheet to another

**What to do**
- Begin with the file outlined in Address Label Generator 1. Double-click on the sheet tab and rename it 'address labels'.
- If there isn't already a blank worksheet in the file, add one by going to the **Insert** menu and clicking on **Sheet**. Double-click on the new sheet tab and rename it 'addresses'.
- Select the 'addresses' sheet and widen columns A to E to about 160 pixels.
- On the addresses sheet, label cell A1 'Name', and B1 'address line 1'. Drag across on B1's *fill handle* to label C1 and D1. Label E1 'Postcode'. Embolden the headings and put borders around them.
- Input several names and addresses, real or imaginary, using one row for each.
- Colour rows 19 and 21 across columns A to E. Label A19 'Copying row'.
- Highlight a row of data by clicking on its row number and [Ctrl] *drag* a copy down into row 20, between the two coloured guide rows.
- Select the 'address labels' sheet and unprotect it (follow **Protect sheet** instructions given in Address Label Generator 1).
- Replace the contents of A1 with the formula **=addresses!A20**. As you do so, the name copied to A20 on the 'addresses' sheet will appear.
- Use A1's *fill handle* to copy the formula into cells A2

to A5. Edit each of these references so that A2 refers to B20; A3 to C20; A4 to D20; and A5 to E20. As you edit each of these, another line of the address will appear.

- Protect the 'address labels' sheet as described in Address Label Generator 1.
- To create a sheet of labels for someone else, simply go to the 'addresses' sheet and copy their data row down into row 20.

### Variations

Make the appearance of the address sheet more attractive using coloured cells and text.

# SECTION 3
# Using Internet Search Engines

Given the rate of development and evolution of search engines it would be foolish to give precise instructions on how to use them. The results of searches using different engines will vary, though the bulk of results will be the same.

Most search engines have similar features, such as advanced search options; Google and Yahoo are good examples. Some search engines can be even more precise, such as Mirago.co.uk, which enables you to restrict your search to a specific region of the UK or even to a county.

An important feature of all search engines is the option to filter results to exclude certain types of website. Usually, the default setting is some level of filtering; but this can be disabled or changed through the 'preferences' part of the search page.

School networks are, as a rule, 'protected' by a filtering service provided by the service provider. However, filters cannot block out all inappropriate search results or pages. Filtering services rely in part on sites being reported to them. This places a responsibility on education professionals to report such sites. If no-one takes the trouble to do so, they will remain accessible on school networks.

Even when a particular page or site has been blocked, that is not the end of the matter. For example, websites which sell explicit videos and trailer them on the internet constantly add new pages to promote their latest release. Using the same search expressions a week or two later will bring up blocked pages and can also include new ones.

The most innocent of searches can produce results you never expected. Here is a classic example and warning: it is unwise to use an advanced Google search for an image of Queen Victoria's husband by title and name unless you use the 'strict filtering' option. If you rely only on Google's 'moderate filtering' option you will get some results more appropriate to a body-piercing establishment than a school or home.

When an innocent search has thrown up explicit material it is probably inevitable that it will be used again with the deliberate intent of revisiting such material. Also, the site which carries the image or material is likely to have more and links to further sites with similar material.

So the message is clear and simple:

- filtering is not infallible;
- pupils in school must not be allowed unsupervised internet access;
- supervising staff must remain vigilant and monitor what is on all screens, including looking on the bottom bar at what may have been minimised for the duration of a supervisor's stroll by.

When inappropriate material appears on a computer screen it is important that you respond in a calm, pre-agreed way. Making a fuss or being shocked does not help, neither does switching off the machine or monitor in question. Your technician needs to be involved in establishing an agreed and measured procedure which should include retrieving the full

URL (Uniform Resource Locator) of the site/pages so that they can be forwarded to your filtering service.

Before you ask your pupils to search for a specific image, it is sensible to try it out first on your network to check that the filtering facilities are effective, particularly where it is possible for users to alter the level of filtering applied by the search engine.

## ADVANCED SEARCHES

A successful search is one which comes up with the information or image required without too many unsuitable results mixed in. Searches sometimes need to be refined to filter out millions of results which, while matching the criteria, do not match the intended purpose. A useful initial refinement maybe to ask for UK sites only.

Using the 'Advanced' search option enables you to target searches more precisely. If you can, use the 'exact phrase' option rather than the standard 'including the words' box. This will define your search more precisely. You can further refine your search by adding more criteria such as 'including the words. . .', 'including any of the words. . .' and 'NOT including the words. . .'. The last option can be good for eliminating spurious results; for example, if you are after pictures of people playing cricket, you can ask for 'NOT including "insect"'.

With image searches, the advanced options usually include choosing image size, file type (useful when looking for photographs) and colour preference (i.e. full colour, monochrome or both).

## COMPARE THE PERFORMANCE OF SEARCH ENGINES

With all the search activities suggested below it is well worth encouraging pupils to use the same search criteria in different search engines, and comparing the number of results each gives. The number of results given could be used as a crude measure of how well a search engine has trawled through the internet; though bear in mind that some engines duplicate search results. Most people settle on using a preferred search engine and often forget that for some searches a different one might give better results.

Consider searching for a company, organisation or service which is available in your locality. Compare the most popular search engines with one such as Mirago.co.uk which specialises in localised searches.

## WEBSITE SEARCHES

- Web search for everyone's everyday 'full name,' 'as a phrase' and as 'all these words'.
  Repeat adding in other names (e.g. middle names) that are normally included. Who has the most results? Which search engine gives you most results? Does everyone have the most results from the same search engine? Who has the fewest results?
  Search for your full name as a phrase, but add in one or two words into the 'all of these' box, such as your location, a hobby, etc.
- Have a race to see who can web search for the website of a particular organisation. Don't choose an easy one where all that's needed is to add the appropriate web suffix.
- Who can be first to find the website of a neighbouring school?

- Animal fact searches – just a few ideas:
  - how much an elephant drinks in a day;
  - how long a sloth sleeps for in a day;
  - how may tigers live in the wild;
  - lifespan of a typical lion in the wild and in captivity;
  - how many eggs a king cobra lays in a clutch;
  - the weight of an average British house sparrow;
  - the number of teeth in a crocodile's mouth;
  - the wingspan of an albatross.
- Geography fact searches – try to relate some to your locality such as:
  - Are there other towns around the world with the same name as your town/nearest town?
  - When was your/nearest town founded?
  - Where is your nearest national park?
  - Where is your nearest reservoir?
  - Market day in. . .;
  - Half-day closing in. . .;
  - The nearest place to buy a yacht or narrowboat;
  - The volume of water in Lake Windermere;
  - The height of Ben Nevis;
  - Where is Loch Carloway?
- Postcode search – put your own postcode into the search 'as a phrase' box and see which addresses close to yours have a presence on the internet.
- People fact searches:
  - Who invented the can opener? (this gives a variety of inventors);
  - Who was the first man to fly a plane non-stop across the Atlantic? (it's not Lindberg);
  - Who is the MP for. . . (anywhere a long way away)?
  - Who is your local mayor?
  - Who is the mayor of. . . (somewhere else)?
  - Name three famous nurses in history;
  - How old is. . . (name of a celebrity)? Where were they born?
  - Search for information on a specific person – what

are they famous for? What is their nationality? When were they born? Are they still alive?

- World records – what is the world record for:
    the heaviest tomato;
    the longest snake;
    the longest jump;
    the quickest mile;
    the fastest train;
    the slowest letter delivery;
    the highest tower;
    the highest bridge.
- Miscellaneous searches:
    What is an awl used for?
    What is a draw knife used for cutting?
    What is the cost of posting a letter in France?
    What is the cheapest way to cross the English
        Channel if you go tomorrow?
    When was the first transatlantic telephone call?
    When was food canning introduced?
    When was the can opener invented?
    What is the price of a humane mousetrap?
    What is the best internet price for a. . . (make
        and model of mobile phone)?
- Search for sound files suitable for adding in to a PowerPoint presentation, such as sounds to accompany animated movements.

## IMAGE SEARCHES

Just because an image is available on the internet do not assume that it is copyright-free. Some sites allow you to download freely and use cliparts for non-commercial use. Photographs are more likely to be 'owned', and permission should be sought before using them. In reality, however, identifying and contacting the owner is not always possible or practical. If you intend to publish an image on your website which has been obtained from another site, you should obtain permission and acknowledge the original webmaster's website.

When selecting an image, take into account the resolution. As a general rule, the larger the file, either in terms of size in pixels or the memory, the better. Images which are too small for your purpose will pixelate if you enlarge them.

When you have double-clicked on the thumbnail and have chosen to see the full-sized image right-click on it and choose either the **Copy image** option or the **Save image as ...** option.

When asking pupils to find an image, be quite precise in what you are asking them to find. Don't just ask for a picture of a cat; specify colour, domesticated or wild, photograph or drawing, file size greater than $n$ KB, etc. You can also specify a location for some searches, perhaps restricting the image search to the local area. These stipulations will encourage the use of more sophisticated advanced search criteria.

### Image search suggestions
(Before trying for any of these, check beforehand that there *is* at least one suitable image to be found. It may be appropriate to turn the search into a race.)

- a drawn clipart of an object or creature;
- a cartoon of someone doing something specific;
- photographs for a schoolwork project, e.g. for a PSHE project on healthy lifestyles, search out images of people exercising, the effects of tobacco, drug and alcohol abuse, 'No Smoking' signs, etc.;
- a photograph of a specific person in the news;
- someone from history – either as a drawing or photograph – are there likely to be colour images of them?
- the inventor of a machine, without naming them –

who invented the computer? (Charles Babbage and his 'difference engine'?);

- people (male or female) carrying out a particular profession;
- people (male or female, young or old) carrying out particular pastimes – angling, metal-detecting, pigeon-racing, re-enacting battles, gardening, jogging, etc.;
- a character from a book or play (Shakespeare?);
- a photograph of a named footballer wearing a particular team strip;
- two named people together;
- someone who has the same name as you;
- someone with the same name as a member of staff;
- a famous landmark;
- a famous building;
- a tourist attraction – Legoland, Disneyland, safari park, holiday centre;
- a holiday destination;
- a geographical feature – hill, valley, escarpment, river, etc.;
- a photograph of a prominent news story/event;
- try an image search using your postcodes as search phrases;
- a civil engineering structure – type of bridge (suspension, cantilever, arched, box girder, etc.), type of power station (nuclear, coal, hydro, wind, wave, etc.);
- a type of building – factory, office block, town hall, shopping centre, place of worship, sports centre, hotel, hospital, concert venue, sports stadium, etc., view of the school;
- a view of a particular city, town or village;
- a child's toy;
- a precise sporting activity – scoring a goal, a hole in one, catching a ball;
- a particular make and model of car, mobile phone, etc.;
- a machine which does a particular job –

commercial bottle-filling machine, baby incubator, etc.;

- a precisely described animal – species, colour (if variable), location (e.g. up a tree), activity (e.g. hunting, feeding);
- an endangered species in its natural habitat;
- food crops being planted, harvested, transported, processed or marketed;
- a manufacturing process – car making, weaving, brewing.

## MISCELLANEOUS INTERNET ACTIVITIES

- Put your postcode into www.multimap.com; find your address and then click for an aerial photograph.
- Go to http://maps.google.co.uk and find where you live. Use the 'Satellite' option and zoom in on your home. This site does not yet have high definition pictures of the whole country so you may instead want to zoom in on London.
- Use the Google Earth program with a broadband link to explore where you live, where you've been on holiday, etc. If you use the search facility for British locations, end the search phrase with UK.

# Short-cut Methods

| | |
|---|---|
| [Ctrl] [Z] | undo |
| [Ctrl] [A] | selects all (e.g. whole of the text in a document, whole spreadsheet, etc.) |
| [Ctrl] [X] | cut to clipboard |
| [Ctrl] [C] | copy to clipboard |
| [Ctrl] [V] | paste from clipboard |
| [Ctrl] [N] | creates a new file |
| [Ctrl] [O] | opens an existing file |
| [Ctrl] [P] | print |
| [Ctrl] [S] | save under existing file name |
| [Ctrl] arrow keys | moves cursor along, one word at a time, in MS Word, PowerPoint and Publisher |
| [Ctrl] backspace delete | deletes one word at a time, in MS Word, PowerPoint and Publisher |
| [Ctrl] drag | copies a selection directly and places it where you release the mouse button |
| [Ctrl] Click | holding down [Ctrl] while you click allows you to select more than one object in many applications |

[Shift] Click

Selecting one object/piece of text, then holding [Shift] and clicking on another, selects all that is between in many applications. For instance, use it to select a large block of text in MS word or a section of a spreadsheet in MS Excel.

# APPENDIX 2
# Windows Paint Tools and Effects

## TOOLS

### Airbrush
The longer you hold down this tool the denser is the spray effect. There are three settings which mimic the effect of the distance of the spray-gun from its target. You can get interesting effects by over-spraying with another colour.

### Brush
There are 12 brush size and shape combinations. Some are excellent for getting into tight corners, especially when used in conjunction with *Magnify*. If your background is still white, you can use a right-click and eraser to correct a slip instead of having to switch to the eraser. You can use this in a sweeping manner with the mouse button held down or for a small, precise area, position the cursor first and then click.

### Curve
You have a choice of line thicknesses. To make a curve you must first of all drag out a straight line, starting and finishing where you want the curve to start and finish. You then have to use two clicking and/or dragging operations. Each of these operations will bend the line towards the cursor position. If you want just one curve, you must click the mouse a second time without moving it.

N.B. If you want to make a second curve straightaway press [Escape] first, otherwise the next line will drag out from where you last clicked for the previous curve.

### Ellipse
Click on the line tool to select the line thickness you want before selecting Ellipse. There are three fill options displayed:
(a) foreground outline with no fill;
(b) foreground outline filled with background (selected by right-clicking on *Color box*); and
(c) solid with the foreground colour.

Holding down [Shift] as you drag out will produce circles rather than ellipses. As you drag out, the dimensions should be displayed at the bottom of the screen.

### Eraser/color eraser
The eraser has four sizes. It can be used in two ways: sweeping with the left-click held down, or careful positioning and using separate, precise clicks. If you are using the sweeping method, it is sensible to intermittently release and reapply the button. If you have to undo a rubbing-out error, it will then only undo what you have erased since the last re-press of the button. If you wish the erased area to be different from the background colour, change it by right-clicking on the *Color box*.

### Fill with color
This fills an enclosed shape with colour. The left mouse button fills using the selected foreground colour while the right click uses the background colour. If there is a gap in the shape, the colour will leak out and fill the whole area. If this happens use [Ctrl] [Z] to undo, then zoom in to find and repair the gap before trying again.

### Free-form select
This enables you to select a non-rectangular part of the screen. It is useful for manoeuvring between sections that are close together and for selecting irregular areas. It can be very useful when you wish to delete part of the image by simply selecting and pressing the [Delete] key.

(See also *Draw opaque* in the section below.)

### Left and right mouse buttons
With all of the drawing tools the left mouse button gives you your foreground colour, selected by left-clicking on the *Color box*. The right click gives you the background colour, white by default. You can, however, change this by right-clicking on the *Color box*. This can be useful if you are predominantly using two colours alternately.

### Line
There are five line thicknesses available. Holding down [Shift] as you drag restricts lines to horizontal, vertical or 45°.

### Magnify
The easiest way of using this is to click-select it then click on the part of the image to be magnified. The other way is to select the tool and click on one of the zoom choices (1x, 2x, 6x, and 8x). The easiest way to leave *Magnify* is to click on the [1x] button.

### Pencil
This is really only for very small area, particularly when used in conjunction with the magnifier to edit part of an image.

### Pick color
This is particularly useful when working with an imported image. It enables you to select a colour that

exactly matches a colour elsewhere in the image. Unfortunately, with composite colours it will only pick up the colour of the pixel it is clicked on. You can then brush, fill, spray, etc.

### Polygon
This tool has the same three fill options as the other shape tools (as described above for *Ellipse*). You can either drag out the sides of the polygon or click where you want the corners, before returning to where you started. To draw a second polygon, re-click on the polygon button first.

### Rectangle
Refer to *Ellipse* for details of the fill options and selecting line thickness. Holding down [Shift] as you drag out will produce squares. As you drag out, the dimensions should be displayed at the bottom of the screen.

### Rounded rectangle
This is the same as *Rectangle* but with rounded corners.

### Select
This is a straightforward rectangular select tool. It can be useful to delete parts of an image (e.g. half a circle) using the [Delete] key.

(See also *Draw opaque* in the section below.)

### Text
When you select this tool you need to drag out a text box. While this box is still selected, the font, size and colour can be changed and the text edited. When you drag out a new text box or choose another tool, it becomes just a part of the image.

## EFFECTS

### Draw opaque

This option comes in to play when you select part of the image. When *Draw opaque* is enabled, the background of the area selected is also selected, forming a (usually white) margin around your chosen section. If you move your selected area, the opaque margin also moves and will cover the image as it is moved over. For normal use it is better to disable *Draw opaque* so that the background of your chosen area is transparent and does not cover other parts of the image when moved. *Draw opaque* can be switched on or off either on the **Image** menu, by ticking/unticking, or by using the two buttons on the toolbar. The toolbar buttons each show a set of 3D shapes, but on one a shape is shown with a white margin around it.

### Flip

To flip part of your image in Paint, select it, then, from the **Image** menu, select **Flip/rotate** and choose the horizontal or vertical option.

### Rotate

In Windows Paint you can rotate a selected part of the image 90°, 180° or 270° clockwise. First select the element using one of the two select tools. Next, click down the **Image** toolbar, click on **Flip/rotate**, select **Rotate by angle** and choose which angle to rotate by. In effect, 90° rotates one right-angle to the right, while 270° rotates one right-angle to the left.

### [Shift] drag

This uses part of your image as a paintbrush. Select part of the image using either of the select tools, hold down the [Shift] key, pause for a moment, then drag.

# Glossary

**Absolute reference** (spreadsheet programs such as Excel)
This is a cell reference in a formula which will not change if moved or copied; for example, where you want to copy a formula across rows or columns but require the reference to remain the same. To create an absolute reference in Excel you insert a $ in front of the cell's letter and number, e.g. **$A$1**. (See also *Relative reference*.)

**Advanced search** (search engines such as Google, Yahoo, etc.)
This search option allows you to be more precise in what you search for, allowing you to use phrases with or without other key words, and to exclude words. For example, while searching for pictures of a cricket match, put 'insect' into the 'Without the words'/'None of these words' option box.

**AutoShapes** (Excel, PowerPoint, Publisher, Word)
These are shapes which can be dragged out on the page. Holding down the [Shift] key has the effect of making them regular.

**AutoSum** (Excel)
This is a spreadsheet tool which allows you to carry out a range of functions, the default one being to total. Click on this button then select the cells you wish to include. To use other AutoSum functions use the drop down arrow next to the button. The 'Average' function can be useful when dealing with a lot of data.

**Character Map**

A program within the Windows operating system which allows you to see, select and copy all font characters including those that do not appear on the keyboard.

**Clipboard**

This is a storage area for text, objects or images which have been *cut* or *copied*. These can then be *pasted* into another file.

**Color box** (Windows Paint)

This is the colour palette which can be hidden or displayed both by the **View** menu and by pressing [Ctrl] [L]. Left-click changes the foreground colour, right-click changes the background colour.

**Connectors** (Excel, PowerPoint, Publisher, Word)

These are lines and arrows (some with curves or right-angles in them) which can be used to connect autoshapes and text boxes together. When applied, connectors will stretch and move when the objects they are connected to move. Connectors are particularly useful for designing and modifying flow charts.

To use a connector select one via the **AutoShapes** button on the **Draw** toolbar. As you move the cursor over an object tiny blue squares appear – these are anchor points for connectors. Click on one, then click on an anchor point on another object. Moving one of the two connected objects will make the connector adjust to retain the connection.

**Copy**

This makes a copy of the selected text, object or image onto the clipboard.

**Copy/paste**

The procedure of copying text or image onto the

*clipboard* with the sole purpose of pasting a copy either elsewhere in the same file or into a different file and/or application. For example, copy a section of a spreadsheet in Excel and paste it (as a table) into a Word document.

**Crop** (Publisher, PowerPoint and some other applications)
This tool is used to crop pictures by cutting from the top, bottom and/or sides. Once a picture has been cropped it can be treated as if the cropping had not taken place.

**Crop handles** (Publisher, PowerPoint and some other applications)
These are the points around the edges of an object (centres and corners) on which you can drag to crop it.

**Custom lists** (Excel)
These are lists of words such as months, days of the week, etc. which can be entered into cells automatically by putting one list item in a cell then dragging on the *fill handle*.

**Cut**
This removes a selection but keeps a copy on the *clipboard*.

**Drag**
To move the mouse with the left button held down.

**Drag on** (various applications)
To place the cursor on a particular point, such as a *handle* on a desktop publishing text box or image, before holding down the mouse button and dragging. This technique is often used for resizing, flipping and rotating objects.

**DTP** (desktop publishing)
Software that enables you to create pages made up of separate objects (e.g. text boxes, images, tables, etc.) which can be mixed and moved about, aligned, etc.

**Fill handle** (Excel)
The bottom right-hand corner of a selected cell or block of selected cells which, when dragged on, allows you to copy or replicate the selected cell(s).

**Flip** (various applications)
This option will flip an object over, horizontally or vertically, so that it becomes symmetrically opposite.

**Group/ungroup**
This feature of Excel, Publisher, PowerPoint and Word allows you to group objects together so that they act as if they are one. You can move, rotate and resize a group. Groups can be ungrouped and the objects selected separately again.

**Handle** (various applications)
Points on an object or selected area of an image, on which you can drag to change its size, shape or orientation, depending upon the type of handle.

**Insert picture** (PowerPoint, Publisher, Word)
This option on the **Insert** menu allows you to insert a picture from any of the following:

- the software's clipart gallery
- a file you have saved on disk or data pen
- direct from a scanner or camera.

**Keyboard shortcuts**
These are key combinations that have the same effect as mouse-clicking on menu items. Most shortcuts involve pressing a letter key while the [Ctrl], [Shift] or [Alt] key is held down.

**Object** (various applications including art and DTP packages)
A component of an image which can be selected separately, such as a picture, wordart, text box, table, etc.

**Paste**
This will paste in the contents of the *clipboard*. In some applications it will only paste in the last object cut/copied to the clipboard. More sophisticated programs store multiple items on the clipboard and allow you to select which you want to paste.

**Print screen**
This is a key which captures an image of the entire screen. See section in 'Some Helpful Hints' in the Introduction for more information.

**Relative reference** (spreadsheet programs such as Excel)
This is a cell reference in a formula which will change automatically if moved or copied. For example, when you want to copy a formula to total a column across rows, the cell references will change for each column, avoiding the need to edit the formula. Cell references in Excel are all relative references when expressed with just column letter and row number, e.g. **A1**. (See also *Absolute reference*.)

**Rotate**
This function in a number of applications allows you to turn an object. The effect is different to flipping an object over. Some programs (such as Paint) only allow rotation in right-angles, while others allow you to rotate freely.

**Rotate handle**
This is a handle on an object on which you can drag in order to freely rotate it. In Publisher and PowerPoint the rotate handle is green.

### Select all

Depending upon the type of software, choosing this from the **Edit** menu, or by using the [Ctrl] [A] shortcut selects:

- all the objects
- all the text
- all the image
- all the spreadsheet cells.

### Select box (Windows Paint)

This is the frame which appears around elements of an image when you have either dragged the *select* tool across or gone around the edge using the *Free-form select* tool. By placing the cursor over the select box you can move the selection using drag. The select box has handles at the corners and in the centre of each side which allow you to resize and stretch the selection.

### Skew handle (PowerPoint and Publisher)

This is the yellow, diamond-shaped handle which allows you to adjust some autoshapes.

### Stack(ing) objects (some DTP and presentation programs, e.g. Publisher, PowerPoint)

When objects are added in, by copying or insertion, they are 'stacked' in layers, the last one being on top. This is only noticeable when they overlap. You can move positions of objects in the stack.

### Text box (various spreadsheet, DTP and word processing applications)

This is a box to contain text which is dragged out and can be resized and background-coloured. Text within the box can be formatted as if in a straight-forward WP program.

### WP (word processor)

Dedicated text software.